Overcoming
7 Deadly Sins
of Trading

Ruth Barrons Roosevelt

Traders Press, Inc.®
PO Box 6206
Greenville, SC 29606

Serving Traders Since 1975

Teresa Darty Alligood
Editing, Layout, and Cover Design
Traders Press, Inc.®

Traders Press, Inc.®
PO Box 6206
Greenville, SC 29606

To my son Graham, who taught me to only play a winning hand!

About the Author

Ruth Barrons Roosevelt coaches traders around the world to trading excellence. She is exceptionally well qualified to offer such guidance to traders, as she herself has extensive trading experience and is to this day an active trader. Her trading experience covers multiple time frames in virtually every futures market, mutual funds, and intense intraday trading in S&P's, T-Bonds, and currencies. She has extensive experience in the brokerage industry in sales and in management, and is a graduate of law school. She has appeared on numerous national and international television programs and has lecutred widely at investment seminars and conferences. Her articles on the psychology of successful trading in many investment publications are well respected. She works with Wall Street professionals as well as individual traders to help them achieve their optimal effectiveness.

Publisher's Foreword

I have often encountered the saying that "Trading is simple, but it is not easy." Reflection on what this implies leads me to believe that it refers to the fact that many of the basic principles of trading are straightforward and easily understood, things like trendlines, moving averages, and the like. The aspect of trading which is NOT easy, and which is not so easily grasped and understood, is the mental or psychological side of trading. The factors that are discussed in this book are the most important components of this facet of trading.

Ruth Barrons Roosevelt, herself a longtime trader who has learned to deal with each of these "deadly sins of trading," shows you in this valuable book how to recognize and overcome these obstacles to the achievement of consistently successful trading habits.

This is Ruth's third book, and it adds to the other valuable contributions she has made to the literature on the psychology of trading. Readers who find this material helpful will also want to avail themselves of the expert guidance Ruth provides in *Exceptional Trading: The Mind Game* and in *12 Habitudes of Highly Successful Traders*. Each of these is available on **http://www.traderspress.com.**

Edward D. Dobson

Edward D. Dobson, President   December 4, 2003
Traders Press, Inc.©
Greenville, SC

TABLE OF CONTENTS

Preface
Introduction

Chapter One
OVERCOMING THE SIN OF FEAR

The Most Ubiquitous of Trading Emotions. A Future Based Emotion. The Choice: Fear or Excitement. The Importance of a Sense of Control. Fear vs. Intuition. Fear as Protection. The Responses to Fear: Flight, Fight, and Freeze-up. Desire Replacing Fear. Accepting Your Emotions and Acting Anyway. Courage Overcoming Fear. Creating and Uncreating Fear. Minimizing Fear to Caution. Mental Clarity as Antidote to Fear. Don't Fear What You Can Do Nothing About. Confidence not Fear. Allowing in the Love of Trading. An Exercise: Circle of Power. Taking a Fear Inventory and Adjusting. Supportive Beliefs.

Chapter Two
OVERCOMING THE SIN OF GREED

The Conundrum Between Risk and Opportunity. Some Examples of Greedy Behavior. Positive Aspects of Greed. How Greed Blinds Us. Some Costs of Greed. The Notion of Scarcity. The Notion of Grandiosity. A Look at a Greedy Trader. Dueling Consequences. How Greed Distorts Perception. The Issue of the Random Event. An Antidote to Greed. Assessing Your Place in the Universe. Taking Inventory and Adjusting. Supportive Beliefs.

Chapter Three
OVERCOMING THE SIN OF RECKLESSNESS

The Difference Between Risk Taking and Recklessness. The Dangers of Nothing More to Lose. Excitement Seeking. The Relationship Between Excitement and Anxiety. Protective Frames: Confidence, Safety-Zone, Detachment. Gambling as Recklessness. A Look at a Reckless Trader. The Many Forms of Recklessness. Some Considerations of Your Own Recklessness. Supportive Beliefs.

Chapter Four
OVERCOMING THE SIN OF PERFECTIONISM

Trading is Not a Game of Perfect. Some Examples of How Trying to be Perfect Backfires. An Impossible Task. Approximations Not Exactitude. The Origins of Perfectionism. Internal Critic. Anger. The Fear. The Disrupting Need to be Right. The Best You Can Do. Self-Acceptance. Self-Appreciation Engenders Self Esteem. Giving Up the Need to Control the Future. The Importance of Curiosity. The Big Picture and the Significant Detail. Recognizing the Goodness Within. Assessing Your Relationship with Perfectionism. Supportive Beliefs.

Chapter Five
OVERCOMING THE SIN OF PRIDE

Attaching your Ego to the Event or Situation Instead of Just Doing your Best. Two Faces of Pride: Hubris and the Effort to Mask Self-Doubt. A Look at an Arrogant Trader. Pride as Ego Pretension. Optimistic Confidence, Not Pride, is What You Want. The Significance of Positive Self-Expectancy. The Importance of a Healthy Self Image. Pride Interferes with Clarity. Pride Obscures Intuition. Loss Aversion. The Endowment Effect. Overconfidence. Under Confidence. An Open Mind. Appraising your Trading Relationship to Pride. Supportive Beliefs.

Chapter Six
OVERCOMING THE SIN OF ANGER

A Destructive Emotion Ubiquitous to Trading. Useful Purposes of Anger. Taking Effective and Reasonable Action. Becoming Aware of your Anger. Shifting Anger to Curiosity. Taking Timely Action. Looking at the Big Picture. Emotions: the Body's Response to Thoughts. The Physiological Consequences of Anger. Losing Control in an Attempt to Gain Control. A Look at an Angry Trader. Moving from Blame to Responsibility. The Money Manager and the Analyst. It's Not Personal. Fighting the Market. Forgiveness as Antidote to Anger. Anger into Learning. Some Steps to Calm Anger. Evaluating Your Tendency to Anger. Supportive Beliefs.

Chapter Seven
OVERCOMING THE SIN OF IMPATIENCE

A Common Trader Trait. A Look at an Impatient Trader. Jumping on the Tiger's Back. Myriad Motivations. Learning to Wait. The Notion of Scarcity behind Impatience. Rushing to Disaster. Seven C's for Timeliness: Clarity, Calm, Consistency, Courage, Caution, Commitment, and Confidence. Assessing Your Level of Impatience. Supportive Beliefs.

Chapter Eight
IDENTIFYING YOUR OWN MAJOR TRADING SINS

A List of Negative Trading Behaviors. Your Personal Seven Deadly Behaviors. Destructive Attitudes and Emotions Underlie Negative Behavior. Possible Harmful Dispositions of Mind and Feeling. Your Personal Seven Deadly Sins. Preferred Trading Behaviors. Supportive Positive Emotions. Supportive Positive Beliefs. Creating a Vision of Your Trading Future.

Chapter Nine
THE BALANCING ACT

Superb Trading Is a Moderating and Balancing of Many Attributes. A Look at the Many Qualities of a Model Trader and How He/She Balances Them. Supportive Beliefs.

OVERCOMING 7 DEADLY SINS OF TRADING

Ruth Barrons Roosevelt

PREFACE

As traders we all do things that keep us from optimal profitability. Underlying these actions are certain emotional attitudes that cause obstructive behavior. At the time we act, we believe we are acting in our own best interests, and yet we are not. Later we may decide we'll never do that again. And yet we do. We do it again and again, and it usually doesn't serve us.

This book identifies seven dispositions that impede trading profitability. It's not enough to identify the behaviors and proclivities that are interfering with your best trading results. You need to change them.

The good news is that you can correct the attitudes and actions that are getting in your way. *Overcoming 7 Deadly Sins of Trading* will help you identify your own unsound practices and the beliefs and feelings that motivate them. You will then be guided in a course of action that will shift your innate impulses to those that will engender effective trading behavior.

You are not alone. Most traders occasionally sabotage their best results. In this book you will be able to experience—and learn from—the mistakes of other traders. This book can be a boot camp for your trading mind.

INTRODUCTION

I have selected seven attitudes that could be ruinous to your trading, and I have called them Seven Deadly Sins. Each of these dispositions of mind may or may not be central to your trading. If you don't commit any of these sins, consider yourself blessed. And look for those habitual modes of thought you do have that hamper your trading. If you are guilty of any of these particular sins, well, remember there is redemption from sins. You can change.

The word sin as I have used it simply means a transgression from good trading principles. I do not mean to use it in any religious sense. If you do commit these trading sins, however, you may well get religion. The attitudes we hold as we trade can make the difference between profitability and loss and between a joyful experience or misery. It all begins with you.

The number seven throughout history seems to be significant. There are the seven days of the week, perhaps springing from the seven days of creation. There are the seven wonders of the world, the seven seas, and the seven heavens. There are seven different notes in a scale, seven colors in the rainbow, sounds and sight parsing into seven. In addition, there are seven sacraments, seven churches of Rome, seven churches of Asia, seven counsels, seven apostles of Spain, and seven deacons. Sevens even enter children's literature. Remember the Seven Dwarfs.

And, of course, we have the seven deadly sins. Take a moment and see if you can remember what they are. It's always interesting to me to note which sins people remember. A young man remembers lust; a fat woman remembers gluttony; and so forth. Well, here they are: pride, covetousness, lust, anger, gluttony, envy, and sloth.

Not as well known as the seven sins are the seven gifts. These are wisdom, understanding, counsel, fortitude, knowledge, piety, and fear of the Lord.

Both the traditional gifts and sins could help and hurt you with your trading. Surely, wisdom, understanding, counsel, fortitude, and knowledge would be a boon to any trader. Pride, covetousness, lust, anger, gluttony, envy, and sloth could be huge barriers to successful trading.

The seven deadly sins of trading I have chosen to address are fear, greed, recklessness, perfectionism, pride, anger, and impatience. To be sure there are more trading sins than these seven. Each trader has his own peculiar blend of trading frailties, and we'll look at some of these as well.

Trading sins are not deadly in the sense that they are fatal. You can overcome the conditions, and we'll be talking about gifts that can replace the sins. This is a book about recognition and change. We're seeking triumph, not despair.

Traders can rejoice when they identify a weakness, because it means that they can strengthen that part of themselves. People think about what they do, and they think about how they feel. Rarely, however, do they think about how they think or what they think about. This book will get you thinking about how to think while you're trading. And you may be surprised and delighted to discover how this benefits the trading process.

Chapter 1

OVERCOMING THE SIN OF FEAR

"Applying fears to hopes, and hopes to fears,
Still losing when I saw myself to win!"
—William Shakespeare

Fear in its myriad forms is the most ubiquitous of the trading emotions, followed in a close second by its partner, greed. So common are these two emotions that they have become cliches to represent in simplicity the whole of the complex trading experience.

What do we fear? We fear everything from small losses to total financial ruination. We fear failure. We even fear success. We fear being wrong, and sometimes we fear that we're right. We fear the unknown, and in trading everything is unknown because the future is not knowable. We fear the news, and we fear there will be no news. We know that the wildness lies in wait, and we fear whatever form it may take. We fear that if we lose, we will lose the respect of our colleagues, bosses, spouses, parents, or friends, or worse still, our own self-esteem. In short, we are afraid or we're afraid we'll become afraid.

Fear is a debilitating emotion. We avoid the things we fear, and in that failure to confront, we can begin to fantasize all kinds of terrible things happening. It weakens our resolve, and in so doing, it weakens ourselves. Fear feeds upon itself. By behaving in a timid way, we increase our uneasiness. On and on in an endless cycle.

FUTURE BASED EMOTION

Fear is a future oriented emotion. This puts us in a difficult position because we can only act, or not act, now. We can't act in the future yet. And so, we can't secure the future thing we fear.

We don't fear the past. It's already done, and we can't do anything about it. The results are known, so there's nothing more to fear. What we feel about the past might be regret, remorse, shame, or guilt, but it isn't fear. We might fear the consequences of past actions or of getting caught, or we might be anxious about repeating the past. However, all this would occur in the future.

Fear in the present is fear about the future. The present is within our control and understanding. We fear what's about to happen next. For example, imagine that a man is holding a gun to your head. You might be afraid, but not because of the present. You are afraid because he might pull the trigger, and that will happen in the future. Maybe it's the immediate future, but it's still the future.

We can't make the future absolutely secure because we can only act in the present. Yes, what we do now has an impact on our future, but it does not take full control of the future. Many factors will shift our future. As traders we're always at risk of future occurrences. We can't see those future events: we can only guess at them. We can see probabilities, but we can't see certainties. And that can either be frightening or exciting depending on your view of the future.

THE CHOICE: FEAR OR EXCITEMENT

It's interesting to note that the adrenaline shot that you get when you're frightened is the same adrenaline that you get when you're excited. How you interpret the adrenaline rush you get when you trade has a great deal to do with whether trading is fun or an ordeal. You can be excited because you have a chance to make a lot of money. Or you can be afraid of the possibility of losing money. Both are possibilities, but one (winning) should be a probability. Do you focus on the probability, or do you focus on the possibility?

Whether you focus on possibility of loss or probability of profit may be determined by whether you're optimistic or pessimistic by nature or inclination. It may also depend upon your values—is it more important to you to preserve capital or to grow capital? Is it more important to avoid being wrong or to make money?

Some traders go back and forth between excitement and fear, allowing their emotions to flow back and forth depending on the micro movements of the trade. No wonder they're totally exhausted at the end of the trading day or week. Others experience fear both before they enter a trade and while they're in the trade.

Johan is a brilliant trader. He is a swing trader, going both long and short for one to three days at a time. He's so good at picking trades that he has an on-line newsletter and many followers. He tells them where to buy, what's the target, and where to put their protective stops. He trades his own recommendations.

Confidently he places his trades. But as soon as he gets a little profit and the market pauses or retraces, Johan breaks into a sweat. *It's a very bad thing to lose! Even a profit! Especially a profit!* Johan jumps out of the trade securing his small to medium profit. The readers of his newsletter hang on until they reach the target. Johan is chagrined as his recommendation clears the target easily over the next day or so. Where is Johan's full profit? His mind tells him one thing, but unreasoned fear kills the full potential. He goes back and forth between hope and fear.

Johan is not alone. *"Cut your losses short, and let your profits run,"* is ordinary garden variety market wisdom. And why is it a cliché? Because we often don't do it.

Steve, on the other hand, is unconflicted. Steve begins each day as a floor trader in a heightened state of awareness. For some that same feeling would be interpreted as fear. Steve interprets his heightened alertness as animated delight. It's the same excitement he used to feel as a kid before Christmas. He knew there was something in those packages, he just didn't know what was in them, but he anticipated it would be something wonderful.

Driving to work, Steve has no idea what the day will bring, but he anticipates the possibility of unique opportunities and the chance to make a giant profit. If not the chance of a lifetime, Steve anticipates he'll be able to make at least a moderate profit. The unknowns of the day are thrilling to Steve. His mind focuses on the potential for wealth.

George, also a floor trader, is on the other end of the spectrum. He starts each day in a state of dread. Will he lose money today? What could go wrong? What if he gets on the wrong side of a trade and can't get out? What if he loses the week's profits? What if he has another month like last December? As he drives to work, he feels cold and clammy. What a horrible way to make a living, he thinks. George focuses his mind on the possibilities of disaster. George needs to establish for himself a greater sense of control over his trading and his ability to handle anything that comes up.

IMPORTANCE OF A SENSE OF CONTROL

With technologies for mind development and direction, we can establish control over our thoughts and actions. A sense of control is essential to well being. Having control over our lives may be the highest value in the hierarchy of human needs. Some say it's food or shelter at the top of human needs, but if you analyze it down to its components, what we most need is control over our ability to secure these essentials.

When we feel we have no control, we become fearful. This fear of lack of control can lead to helplessness and depression.

"Anxiety and depression are related in the following way: when a man or animal is confronted with a threat or loss, he responds initially with fear; if he learns that the threat is wholly controllable, fear disappears, having served its function; if he remains uncertain about controllability, fear remains; if he learns or is convinced that the threat is utterly uncontrollable, depression replaces fear." [1]

—Martin Seligman

That's one of the ways terrorists seek to undermine a country. Something dangerous is coming at you over which you have no control. Is it anthrax? Is it small pox? Is it some other form of bioterrorism? Is it airline hijacking? Is it a nuclear device in a suitcase? Will the water or food supply be poisoned? What is next? When you feel you are in danger, and you have no way to protect yourself, you first become frightened, then depressed, then immobilized. This is the plan of terror.

Remember the studies of the dogs who learned helplessness. They were locked in cages and given repeated shocks. First they tried to get away. After they learned they were powerless to escape, they lay down and accepted the inevitability of the shocks. Later when the cages were opened, and they could jump out and escape the shock, they didn't try. They lay there as if they were still helpless. They had given up.

We need to take control of what we can control, and then detach from what we cannot control.

Fortunately, as traders we do have control. We don't have control over news or market prices, but we definitely have control over how we react to events and prices. We can always respond to whatever happens to protect ourselves.

Some traders do not, and apparently cannot, control their own reactions. Others don't know whether or not they will take disciplined action when things don't go their way—or even when they do go their way. These traders are indeed out of control, and their fear is well placed.

Some traders caught in fear and resulting undisciplined behavior begin to interpret their trading as being uncontrollable. After a while, their fear can turn into listless depression. At this point many will stop trading completely.

They are not simply taking a well-deserved trading vacation; they are giving up. A sense of helplessness overcomes them. If and when these folks decide to go back to trading, the past will very likely repeat itself unless they have done self change work on a deep level.

Through shifting beliefs and values and learning techniques for establishing focus and appropriate interpretation, they will be able to develop mastery over themselves, and return to trading with a new sense of control.

FEAR VS. INTUITION

It has been said that fear (F.E.A.R.) is False Expectations Appearing Real. It could also be said that fear is Fateful or Factual Expectations Appearing Real. Whether what we fear is a false expectation (a fearful thought not based on evidence) or an intuition of what could happen (a warning based on conscious or unconscious evidence) makes a significant difference. But it is often hard to tell the difference.

One person's intuition is another person's fear. When you hear that voice inside of you saying, "Don't do it," you have been presented with a warning. Is it merely idle, disruptive fear, or is it your unconscious mind telling you that something isn't right?

To tell the difference between intuition and gratuitous fear, you can start making notes at the time. Do you see a picture? Do you say something to yourself? Is it your voice or is it someone else's voice? Is it a feeling you get? What kind of a feeling is it? When you have sufficient history as to how you receive warnings and which particular types of warnings turn out to be predictive and which are simply unfounded fears, you may decide to act on some premonitions and to dismiss others.

For example, if as you look at a chart, you imagine it changing direction and it does change direction subsequently, make a note. The next time that happens, again record whether or not the imagination is followed by reality. If you say, "This market's going to change," but it doesn't, record that. When you feel in your stomach that the trade is going to sour on you, record whether or not it does go against you. You will soon get a sense as to how your intuition speaks to you. For many of us fear and intuition speak in different ways, and we can begin to trust our reactions.

I knew a psychic who had an uncanny way of actually predicting future events. You may or may not believe in psychic accuracy or possibility. However, this woman predicted events in my life that she could not possibly have grasped through normal channels of knowing. She had learned to trust the accuracy of her information depending on how she received it. When she saw a picture, it might or might not be accurate; but when she heard a voice in her left ear, she trusted it. According to her, we all receive certain psychic information, but we don't know how to recognize it. She learned what to trust through trial and error. Hers was auditory on the left side. Others may get pictures or feelings.

Of course, when we speak of intuition, we're not speaking of psychic knowledge. We're speaking of something the unconscious mind recognizes over and above our left brain analytical conscious thinking. As traders we spend hours and hours observing how markets behave, and we really do know more than we know we know.

Intuition is NOT the analytic mind making decisions. Intuition is a communication from the unconscious mind. The conscious mind embraces what you are actually thinking at that moment. Everything else is unconscious. Because our conscious mind can only handle five to nine items at a time, the unconscious mind plays a huge role in our observations and decisions. You can think of your unconscious mind as your partner in success.

Keep in mind, however, intuition is not always correct. That feeling in your gut, be it fear or intuition, may very well be mistaken. Intuition is true, but it may not be accurate. The market has unique ways of being deceptive, misleading, shifting, or suddenly arbitrary. Some people do have highly accurate feelings about what the market will do, and they can trust their intuitions. Others seem to intuit the exact opposite of what the market will do, and these people are better off strictly following their technical strategies.

Through time you can also begin to note the difference between simple fear itself and fear based on significant market action. There are times you want to be warned. You can begin to distinguish between price movement that is predictive and price movement that is simple meandering noise.

FEAR AS PROTECTION

Remember fear serves a valuable purpose. Without fear the baby will put her hand on the hot stove or chew on the electric cord. Without fear the child runs into the street in front of a speeding car. Without fear the eager young investor risks all his capital on one compelling idea. Without fear the novice trader just keeps popping into the market to see what will happen next.

Fear gives us an important message that we need to take care—that there's something in our future for which we need to prepare or from which we need to protect ourselves. That takes us to the next point as to how much fear is useful and what degree of fear is destructive and even more dangerous than the thing we fear.

I've been using the word fear over and over as a generic—as in fear and greed. But there are many types and degrees of fear. There is dread, panic, fright, and terror on the extreme high side going all the way down to concern or uneasiness on the low side. In between are nervousness, anxiety, agitation, hesitation, irresolution, pusillanimity, and timorousness.

Most traders—unlike business people—are willing to admit to any of the above degrees of fear that they feel. Business people will usually only refer to stress, or at worst, burnout. But whatever you call it, it's an unpleasant feeling that registers in the body in anticipation of, or awareness of, impending danger. The danger may be real or imagined.

"And I will show you something different from either Your shadow at morning striding behind you Or your shadow at evening rising to meet you I will show you fear in a handful of dust.
— T.S. Eliot

What you do in response to the feeling is what makes or breaks your trading. Typical responses to fear can be categorized under **flight, fight, and freeze-up**.

"No passion so effectually robs the mind of all its powers of acting and reasoning as fear."
—Edmund Burke

SOME RESPONSES TO FEAR

FLIGHT

Maryanne has a highly effective S & P day trading system. Unfortunately, she's not profiting from it. She sits there day after day watching the screen, recording the trades on paper. Each day she thinks she'll trade; but when the signals come up she simply writes them down. She busies herself so she doesn't have to experience risk.

Maryanne is running out of money. It takes funds to sit there day after day doing nothing to earn a living. It would appear that she's more afraid of losing money than she is of not making money. She flies away from opportunity because she sees it as danger.

Johan also flies away from the opportunity to gain large profits by jumping out of his trades at the first wiggle against him. Day after day he gets jiggled out of his big reward.

FIGHT

Robert fights for all he's worth to turn a losing trade into a winner. Instead of just getting out when the trade goes against him, he digs in. He may double the position and double it again. Anything to turn this loser into a winner! Sometimes he fights his way out and thinks he's done a good thing. But on those trades where he doesn't work his way out, he takes enormous hits.

Sometimes Robert will just take the loss, but then he fights to make it back immediately. As the day goes by he trades larger and larger to make up the accumulating deficits. He digs his hole deeper and deeper. Succeed or fail, at the end of the trading day, Robert is exhausted from the struggle. The try, try, try again doesn't work for Robert in the trading arena. How could it? He's struggling with the same unsuccessful strategies.

It's sad because fight to succeed works in many other areas of Robert's life. Plain old harder and harder effort will work if you're mopping a floor or mowing a field. It doesn't help in trading. Robert needs to work smarter, not harder.

FREEZE-UP

It had never happened to him before. When it did happen, it was frightening because it was so unprofessional and potentially hazardous. Fred traded options on the CBOE. He was short thousands of calls when the Fed unexpectedly lowered the discount rate. The market soared and the price of the calls went through the roof. Stunned and horrified, Fred simply stood there. Time passed. He broke into a cold sweat and his head felt light. He was facing ruin and he couldn't move.

26

Fortunately the market began to recede and the calls deflated somewhat. Fred was finally able to take action and scramble out of his position. It left him feeling vulnerable knowing that he could freeze in the face of a sudden reversal.

DESIRE REPLACING FEAR

One of the antidotes to fear is desire. Desire directs the focus of the mind away from what we don't want to happen to what we do want to happen.

> *"It is a miserable state of mind to have few things to desire and many things to fear."*
> —Francis Bacon

Since our emotions are a response to a thought, what we focus our attention on creates a corresponding emotion. Our focus can create boredom or curiosity, regret or commitment, sorrow or gratitude, criticism or forgiveness, excitement or anxiety, and so forth.

There are many ways to direct our focus. Perhaps the easiest way is to select the questions we ask ourselves. Questions not only change the direction of thought, they presume the underlying truth of the question.

Mary Nathan had been taught by her mentor a powerfully effective method for trading the currencies. She studied the process and paper traded it. The results were extraordinarily profitable—on paper that is.

When it came time to go real time, Mary became overly nervous. Not surprisingly, her first trade contained an error. She sold short the Swiss Franc. When she received a signal to cover the trade, she sold again. (This is a common error for new traders seeking to get out of a short position. After all, if you want to get rid of something, you sell it. Not when you're short, you don't!)

As the trade was coming to an end, and the direction of the trade was reversing, Mary doubled her position. And she didn't even know it! By the time she discovered her mistake, Mary's profit had become a loss. Naturally, this unnerved her.

Thereafter when she went to trade, Mary would hear a little voice asking, "What if you lose?" The question was asked, and she had to follow it. She would go all the way to the end of the trade and feel the pain of losing. In her imagination she actually experienced the loss and believed it. The result of all this was that she sat there day after day intending to trade, fully committed to trade, but never doing anything more than paper trading. Because the results of the paper trading were good, Mary felt remorse and guilt for missing out. She became harshly critical of herself. "What's the matter with me?"

Again the question misled her. She went on a hunt for all that was the matter with herself. Daily frustration and self-deprecation reduced her to tears and lowered her self-esteem. Try as she might, she couldn't trade.

Sometimes you can't correct the thing all by yourself. As one of my friends says, "You can't hide your own Easter eggs." In this case, of course, Mary needed to find them.

Mary was determined to trade her system. She wanted very strongly to do it. But she didn't. That's the way it is. When the will seeks to do one thing, and the imagination envisions the opposite, the imagination wins every time. And the stronger the will power, the greater advantage the imagination has.

I taught Mary to change the direction of her imagination by changing the questions she asked herself. When the little voice said, "What if I lose?" I taught her to ask in an even louder voice, "What if I win? What if this trade is a big winner?" At that point, I had her visualize the chart going in the direction of her signal. Instead of feeling the fear of a loss, she began to feel the anticipation of a win. I had guided her through mental exercises and mental rehearsal, and she was able to change the way she felt about her entry signal.

Instead of saying, "What's the matter with me?" I taught her to ask, "How can I get better at this? In what ways am I already getting better?"

Questions direct the focus of the mind. The focus becomes the reality. Mary changed fear to desire. Mary began to trade, and trade profitably.

ACCEPTING YOUR EMOTIONS AND ACTING ANYWAY

"Whether fear is your friend or foe depends on whether you become its master or its servant."
—Dan Millman

Emotions are a natural response to a thought or perception. In a sense, emotions are as natural as weather. We accept the weather, good or bad, and we can accept emotions, comfortable or uncomfortable. True, we can change what we focus on and change our thoughts and their accompanying emotions. We can change the interpretation we give to events and perceptions, and alter our feelings. But in simply trying to suppress an emotion, we really haven't changed it. It remains with us to effect our trading.

Emotions just are. We cannot deny or repress them, or they will get the better of us in the long run. We can accept them with the same grace with which we accept the weather. We need to acknowledge what we're feeling.

You're feeling fear? Okay. Fear has its own message. Accept the fear. Fear is a message that there is something in the future that needs to be prepared for. Now, when your methods tell you it's time to enter the market or exit the market, you have already prepared for this circumstance. You know already what is *probably* best to do.

"Do the thing you fear and the death of fear is certain."
—Ralph Waldo Emerson

It is time to take action. You need to take the action that your guidelines tell you to take—***whether or not you feel like it.*** Fear can freeze you in or out of a trade; fear can make you jump out of a trade when it's just getting going; fear can make you fight the tape. These are not right actions. Right action is following your game plan. Right action is adhering to your trading rules. Right action is doing what you might fear to do.

Action has a way of quelling fear. The more disciplined action you take when confronted with fear, the easier it is to take action the next time, and the next time. With time and the repeated experience of taking action in the face of fear, the intensity of the emotion diminishes. Action is your greatest weapon for overcoming fear. Action teaches you courage. Courage becomes your automatic response to fear in trading.

COURAGE OVERCOMING FEAR

"Many of our fears are tissue-paper thin, and a single courageous step would carry us clear through them."
—Brendan Francis

Courage doesn't mean not being afraid. Courage involves feeling the fear and acting anyway. It means managing the uncertainties with bravery and backbone. By taking courageous action, you begin to reverse the cycle of fear.

Courage is contagious. One act of daring is followed by another and another and another. It becomes a style of trading. You act in the moment. You push on through to the thing you want. Ultimately, it boils down to execution. You decide, and you facilitate. You focus on the probabilities of your methods, and you execute them within the market. The last thing you want to do is think yourself into paralysis.

Don't let yourself get caught up in uncertainties, in what might happen to derail the trade. Once again, use useful questions. "What does my system tell me to do?" "What is the market doing?" "What is the trend?" "Where is the next trade?"

Courage is habit forming. The more you act with pluck, the easier it is to do it the next time. When you step right in at the appropriate time, and you are rewarded by it, it becomes a memory that propels you into the next high probability trade. When you exercise courage, you also exercise your mental muscles for valor and boldness. You become stronger, and it becomes easier to focus on your plan and execute that plan.

FEAR IS CREATED AND IT CAN BE UNCREATED

How we think has a large effect upon what we fear and whether we fear at all. It's easy to turn possibilities into probabilities, but this is a major mistake. Sure, it's possible your house could burn down. It's possible your dog could get run over. It's possible you could get mugged on the street. It's possible a terrorist could wipe out your town. It's possible you could get cancer. But it's not probable. Yes, it's possible you could lose all your trading capital and be forced to stop trading. But it's not probable as long as you follow good trading principles and solid risk and money management.

When you catch yourself catastrophizing by turning possibilities into probabilities, STOP! Take a deep breath. Break the connection. Then ask yourself, "Is this probable?" Continue to challenge the thought by asking, "What are the probabilities right now?" Then choose to take control of your thoughts and think in terms of the current probabilities.

MINIMIZING FEAR TO CAUTION

A young trader came to see me at lunchtime, wearing his cap backwards, and eating a slice of pizza. "My gosh, Ruth," he said, "I'm fearless, and that scares me to death. I could lose all my capital!"

Truth be told, he could. Trading without caution is a dangerous thing. "How can we add caution to your trading?" I asked. "What rules or guidelines can we write that will protect you?"

Others are so filled with caution that it amounts to a preoccupation, and that preoccupation develops into full fledged fear. These people need to reduce the fear to caution. They too can develop caution by writing protective guidelines for money and risk management. With appropriate rules they can turn their worry over to the guidelines that they have built into their trading to protect themselves.

You can look at protective stops and money management rules as an insurance policy. Naturally, you don't want your house to burn down, but you're sure glad you've got fire insurance. Of course, being a mentally healthy person, you don't sit around thinking what would happen if your house should burn down. You've taken a precaution, and you forget about it. After all, an ounce of precaution is worth a pound of cure. And it's also worth a pound of fear.

MENTAL CLARITY AS ANTIDOTE TO FEAR

When you think clearly about your trading, you put yourself into a position to win. You find out what works, you verify that it does work, and then you execute it smoothly.

There is, after all, no need to fear the probabilities of winning. There's every reason to rejoice. When through clear thinking and testing both forward in time and historically, you have a plan that will *probably* make money over time, you have nothing to fear—just the small possibility of loss. And you accept that possibility, and move on.

You are motivated. You WANT TO make money trading. You believe that your goal is achievable and worthwhile. You believe money can be made in the markets. It can be done. It's possible.

You have the means. You know HOW TO trade. You have taken the physical and mental steps necessary to put yourself in a position to trade profitably. You know how to read the market. You can deal effectively with whatever comes up. You believe you can make money in the markets. You can do it. You're capable.

You have the opportunity. You have the CHANCE TO make money. You can deal effectively with inner and outer interference. You feel you are worthy of making money. You understand money is good and is good for you. You believe that you deserve to make money in the markets. You deserve to do it. You're worthy.

WHY FEAR WHAT YOU CAN DO NOTHING ABOUT?

"There is hardly anything productive about worry or fear when you can't do anything about the circumstances."
—Buzz Aldrin

You have decided to trade a particular system. You get an entry signal, and you put on the trade. You put in your protective stop, and you know what will be your signal or target for exit. There's nothing more to do. The market will do the rest. You are along for the ride, and you know when to get out. Why be anxious?

The more you do this, the easier it gets. Trading is just living your life, and going through your working day. Each day you get stronger.

Buzz Aldrin put it this way: "I don't think anybody—astronauts or otherwise—is born with some kind of right stuff. It's something you work into. You don't learn it, but you adjust to it in your own way. Or else you wash out of flight school and get a job as a journalist."

Sure, you could stop trading and go get a job selling used cars or writing ad copy. But that's not what you want to do. You want to trade, and you can. You can grow into it.

CONFIDENCE NOT FEAR

"In quietness and confidence shall be your strength."
—The Bible

In any situation where you are confident, there is no need for fear. The one replaces the other. Confidence is a firm trust in yourself and your ability to handle a particular situation.

So how does one develop confidence as a trader? Some might say that they need to have an extended period of success trading before they can be confident, and they can't have success until they are confident. These people have put themselves into a double bind.

You break it down into elements. Where do you need more preparation? Do you have enough capital? If not, make a plan to create the capital. Do you have a winning strategy? If not, find or develop one. Do you need more experience trading the market? If you do, start trading in the smallest increment possible—one e-mini or ten shares of stock.

Perhaps you have enough experience trading the market, but you need to develop a history of winning. One way to do this is through mental rehearsal. In mental rehearsal, it's easy to do the right thing at the right time right on time. Mentally rehearse your trading. Do it consistently and repeatedly.

Another way to build confidence in yourself as a trader is to treat yourself the same way you would treat a child in whom you wished to develop a secure sense of self.

With a child, you criticize the act and not the person. Johnny did a bad thing. And he can stop doing that. Not, Johnny is a bad boy. Stop telling yourself you're an idiot because of the way you trade.

You use mistakes as building blocks for learning. They're simply steps forward in the learning process. You understand that you cannot learn without small failures. If the baby gave up on the first fall, she would never learn to walk. Develop new learnings as you trade. And forgive yourself for your foibles.

You catch yourself doing something right, and you praise it. You praise the child when she's quietly crayoning in her coloring book. "What a good girl! Look at that good work." You don't wait for her to start tearing up the house and then yell at her. What you pay attention to, you get more of.

Pay attention to what you're doing that's working. Begin to appreciate your growing skills as a market person. Questions, once again, will help. "What did I learn today?" "What did I do today that was effective?" "In what ways am I getting to be a better trader?" "How can I become an even better trader?"

ALLOW YOURSELF TO LOVE TRADING

"Fear is the energy which contracts, closes down, draws in, runs, hides, hoards, harms."

"Love is the energy which expands, opens up, sends out, stays, reveals, shares, heals."
—Neale Donald Walsch

If trading is a burdensome, fearsome, unpleasant task for you, by all means, find something else you love to do.

On the other hand, if trading is an exciting and promising enterprise for you, throw yourself into it. Get good at it. Learn, practice (if only with small monetary commitments), and throw yourself into it whole heartedly. Your love of trading will cast out the old and unnecessary fear.

EXERCISE TO CONQUER FEAR IN TRADING

CIRCLE OF POWER

1. Imagine a Circle of Power on the Floor.

2. Step into the Circle of Power.

3. Look outside the circle of power and visualize the resource of infinite potential, that there is unlimited abundance of wealth to be created. Give it a color; for example, green.

4. Turn one quarter around in the circle, and imagine the resource of the capability of identifying opportunity clearly and easily and acting upon it quickly and smoothly. Give it a color; for example, blue.

5. Turn another quarter to halfway around the circle. Picture the resource of discipline, of the ability to consistently follow your trading guidelines. Give it a color; for example, purple.

6. Turn one more quarter. Visualize the power of courage and willingness. Give it a color; for example, red.

7. Turn back to the beginning. Reach out with your hands and pull in the greenness of unlimited abundance and the thought that anything is possible. Center it within yourself.

8. Turn to the blueness of the ability to identify and act upon opportunity. Reach out and pull that within yourself.

9. Turn to the purple of discipline. Bring that within yourself.

10. Turn to the redness of willing courage and courageous willingness. Pull that within yourself

11. Face your original place of unlimited potential. Imagine a circle of golden light above your head. Let that represent your higher self and your connection with the universe. Remember that the markets are part of the universe. Reach up and bring that down within yourself.

12. With a gesture seal these powers within yourself.

13. In your imagination tip your Circle of Power vertically in front of you. Picture it circling around getting brighter and smaller until you can put it on your finger as a ring.

14. Before you trade, throw your Circle of Power around your trading place, and sit right down in it.

TAKING INVENTORY AND ADJUSTING

1. Make a list of the trading actions you take that could be a manifestation of fear.

2. List the actions you would rather take.

3. Name the emotion you would need to feel in order to take these actions consistently.

4. Write down the beliefs you would need to hold in order to feel and act the way you choose.

5. Write these beliefs into well formulated affirmations. An affirmation needs to be stated positively in the present as if it were already true. An affirmation is a statement made in the present about the future as if it had already occurred in the past.

6. Let these affirmations become a part of you. Write them on cards, repeat them, record them, listen to them, incant them, and let them become a natural part of your way of thinking and doing and feeling.

7. Make a mental image of the affirmations already realized.

8. Believe the certainty of your achievement.

SUPPORTIVE BELIEFS

- Losses are a simple cost of doing business.

- Since I always limit my loss to an amount my account can withstand, there is nothing to fear.

- I have the courage to do whatever it takes to succeed at trading.

- Each trade is but one of many.

- I keep my focus in the present because this is where the action is.

- The potential profits are worth the risk.

- Trading is about money: it's not about my survival.

- Trading is only one way in which I can make money.

- I learn and grow stronger with each trading experience.

- The future of my trading is bright.

[1] *Helplessness on Development, Depression & Death,"* Martin E. P. Seligman, W. H. Freeman and Company, ISBN 0-7167-0752-7.

Chapter 2

Overcoming The Sin of Greed

"There are two great mistakes that a trader can make. First, he can lose all of his capital. Second, he can fail to take advantage of an opportunity."
—Roy W. Longstreet

Greed is an inordinate wanting, a longing that is out of control. Greed by its very definition can never be satisfied. You get what you wanted, and you want more. There is never enough. Clearly, this is not a satisfactory situation to be in. You are dissatisfied no matter what happens. It is one thing to be alert to opportunity and take advantage of that opportunity, and it is quite another thing to be greedy. Imagine the following scenarios.

- You've been making money trading your system in the currencies with one contract for each currency. You decide to make more money by trading five contracts. Naturally, you hit a protracted draw down.

- You sell your stock with a decent profit, but it keeps going up. You feel a sickness in the core of your being every time the stock advances. You're so preoccupied, you stop looking for other opportunities.

- Every time you miss a trade for whatever reason, you feel a terrible nervousness. You forget the trades you caught. You keep thinking of the ones that got away. It claws at you.

- You have a loss. You want to make it back. Today. You start grabbing at anything and everything. When that doesn't work, you double your size. You're digging in, and you're digging your hole deeper and deeper. You're determined to get out of this even, but it's going the other way.

- You get a tip from your brother-in-law. You get excited. You don't bother to check it out. You call your broker and buy 1,000 shares. That was the top. The stock goes down from there, but you hold on. It's got to go up.

- You're testing out a system. It looks good. Before you complete the testing, you start trading it real time with real money. Turns out the system doesn't work.

- Your broker calls you with a sure thing. He sells you the sizzle. "What's the price of the stock?" you ask. "You're asking the wrong question." he answers. "You need to ask where is it going?" You do, and you buy, already imagining the stock at the price he predicts.

- You see your neighbor making money trading. It seems so simple. You borrow money so you can do the same thing. Only it doesn't pan out. Now you owe money.

Okay. You didn't do all those things. Of course not. But did you ever do one of them? Or something like it? At that moment you were under the thrall of greed. Inordinate wanting. Unrealistic dreams of glory. You were under the spell of the pied piper of the market.

Okay. You never did any of those things or anything like it. You're free from greed. Don't be so quick with your self-satisfaction. My guess is you're not trading.

It takes a little bit of greed, or at least strong desire, to enter the market with the risk it entails. Without desire, there is no reason to take action. Without strong desire, there is no reason to put your money at risk. You need to be alert to opportunity and act upon it. And so, in some ways, a little bit of greed is good. It gets you moving.

"The point is, ladies and gentlemen, greed is good. Greed works, greed is right...and greed, mark my words, will save not only Telder Paper but the other malfunctioning corporation called the U.S.A."
—Gordon Gekko in "Wall Street"

The total opposite of greed is contentment. If you are content with your capital and the yield it is giving you, why jeopardize it?

This is the conundrum of the trader. To partake in an opportunity, the trader must of necessity stand the chance of losing something he already has. That bird in his hand could fly away while he seeks to capture the two in the bush. But he really wants the two in the bush! Ah, then it's worth trying. But he really wants to keep the one in the hand! Then leave the two in the bush alone.

How foolish the trader feels when he loses the bird in his hand as he rushes the two in the bush. He ends up empty handed and broken hearted. How powerless the trader feels who clutches the bird in the hand while he watches another trader catch two additional birds to make a total of three. He gets trapped in self-recrimination. And that's the game of trading. It really is a matter of nothing ventured, nothing gained. We have to let go of something valuable in order to win something even more valuable. But how much do we venture? Where do we set our limits?

PAUL'S STORY

"It's like I've got a demon in me," Paul said. "I really am possessed. I must have a bad karma from a prior life."

"I trade very well. I can read the charts. I don't have a system or anything like that, but I can see from the charts where the good trades are. It's a wonderful gift. And I make money, and I build it up. I build up the account slowly and carefully. $30,000 becomes $200,000."

"And then it happens, and I give it all back in one trade. I see something in the charts, and I know intuitively that a huge move is coming. I feel a kind of energy—a wild energy filling my body. I say to myself, 'This is going to be the big one, and I'm going to do it.' I load the boat, and I keep loading it as it goes my way. I'm very sure of myself."

"And then something happens, and I lose half of my profits. 'Ah, it'll turn around,' I say. I get stubborn, and I dig in. And slowly but certainly once again, I've lost everything."

"And then I start again, and I build the capital up with careful trading. And then I do it again. It's like watching paint dry. You know it will dry, but you have to touch it while it's still wet. Sure, I've got rules. I've got nine rules and I've got them written all over the place. But I don't follow them. I tell you there's a maniac demon inside me that makes me squander my special gifts."

Greed blinds us. We see only what we want to see. Paul has dug into a scenario. He is telling himself his story. Because he believes his story, he does not put protective limits on his trade. He doesn't give up his profits because he wants to torment himself. No. He wants more, more, more of what he already has. He is convinced he's right. He's hypnotized himself to think that this is the one that will take him over the top. And he doesn't want to let go. He's sort of gotten himself into the position of the monkey who stuck his hand in the bottle to get the banana, but cannot get his hand out because he won't let go of the banana.

Hope combines with greed to keep you in a trade even when you know you should get out. Hope becomes the poor, blind, passive hand maiden of greed. Listen to John's story.

JOHN'S STORY

"I worked carefully day trading all week, and then I blew up the week's profits in one stupid trade. I got locked into a short trade as the market was rushing up. First of all, I was late to the party. The stock had already dropped two points when I got short just 30 cents from the bottom. When it started to go against me, I got stubborn. I didn't want to realize a loss. So I sat there with it the whole day. At end of the day, I still didn't want to take the loss. It's against my rules, but I took the loser home. Of course, Murphy's Law, it gapped up against me on the open. I watched it for a while, and when it started to move up, I finally got out. What a relief! Finally I was free to look for a new trade."

Greed often manifests in the unwillingness to accept and realize a loss.

John, being unwilling to realize a loss, was afraid to give up any of his capital. This comes from a sense of insufficiency. The trader can't accept a real loss, even though it avoids a much greater potential loss. In such a case, not only hope combines with greed, but denial and self delusion enter the mix to prevent the timely exit of the trade.

THE NOTION OF SCARCITY

Most greed comes from a sense of scarcity, the idea that there might not be enough. If a person has a sense of abundance, there is no need to over trade or to greedily hold unto a position hoping for more, more, and more, when the market is signaling the move is over. Nor is there reason to fight loss if there is a sense of potential wealth and opportunity. Nor is there any reason to bemoan money left on the table.

Traders who have a sense of plenty do not experience greed, inordinate longing, or frenzied wanting. Traders who see the world and the markets as abundant with present and future opportunity, do not need to grasp and clutch at the trades. And they do not, because the next opportunity, large or small, is just around the corner.

THE NOTION OF GRANDIOSITY

There is another kind of greed to be distinguished from greed that stems from a sense of insufficiency. It is greed born of grandiosity. A trader arrogantly assumes she can acquire infinitely more because she's done it in the past or she's seen others do it. An easy-come-easy-go attitude is built on the assumption that after the easy-go, the easy-come will naturally recur.

The grandiose attitude goes beyond a comfortable assumption of abundance to a presumption of ease of acquisition. The belief that one has the Midas touch, that one can do no permanent wrong, can cause a trader to over trade or to not protect herself against undue loss of capital. The notion of grandiosity is built upon the belief of personal invincibility. Over confidence and a sense of over deservedness puts the trader out of touch with changing realities. Clear vision and prudent action are lost. Such a trader risks ruin in turbulent or shifting markets.

A GREEDY TRADER

You want to make money. You want to make the right decision. You know that the conundrum of the trader is choosing between a palpable opportunity and protecting your capital. You don't want to overreach, nor do you want to deny yourself the possibility of a large profit.

Gregory Wilson turned his swivel chair away from the computer screen and looked out the floor to ceiling window at the ocean. Wave after wave rolled in. It was high tide. Just like the market, he thought, change and an endless supply of source. How lucky he'd been to build this house and much else with his trading profits.

Everything seemed to work out for Greg. His well toned athletic build, thick blonde hair, and teasing brown eyes fascinated women along with his sense of humor and easy charm. Men also enjoyed his company. He was a good athletic competitor and an easy companion.

Trading came easily to Greg. He had a feel for the markets, and a willingness to act. He was a man of action. He'd weigh the evidence, make a decision, and act upon it. Greg expected to win. His mode of operation was optimistic. He understood at his core the enormous potential for overflowing wealth through trading. He had himself created considerable wealth, and he intended to keep on doing more.

As he watched the waves roll in, he thought of his current position in the market. He was long grains—corn, wheat, and soybeans. As it went his way, he'd been pyramiding more size into his original position which was large even for him. He wasn't top heavy because the original position was so big. He contemplated adding more. This one could put him over the top.

He realized, of course, that this was a weather market. A good strong rain in the Midwest could bring it crashing down on him. He remembered nearly being wiped out once as a weather market reversed. He was lucky that time. It reversed back his way, and he'd been able to get out with a sizable profit instead of an annoying loss.

This was a major opportunity. He could read it in the charts and feel it in his bones. Would he be overreaching if he added? It was a fine line between courting disaster and skimping on the trade of the year. He didn't want to be blindsided by white hot desire, nor did he want to cower in the face of uncertainty. A trader makes his living by taking chances. Greg added to the position.

The markets closed. Greg felt vindicated. The grains continued to rise—even after he had added the last batch of contracts. You don't get anywhere without real risk. He called his friend, Fred.

"Hey, man, isn't this the greatest? These babies are going to the moon."

"Yeah, man, this one is going to be huge."

They were each of them preaching to the choir. They were both long, having bought expecting the market to go higher. They were both convinced.

He slept that night with an easy confidence. He'd ride this one to the end. That was how you made the big money. That morning the grains opened up and continued up. Oh sure, there were a couple of wiggles during the day, but he knew how to ride out minor reversals.

That night he called his friend John in Chicago. Something was beginning to make him uncomfortable.

"Hey, man, have I got my head screwed on right? Is this thing really going to run big, or is it just a fool's paradise?"

"Greg, I think so. It looks like this is going to be like the old days. Remember 'beans in the teens' when the soybeans kept going up and up?"

You know that every single time you enter or exit a market, there are at least two possible consequences. How you think at that moment, which emotion dominates your thoughts and actions carries enormous consequences. A little overconfidence, a small dash of grandiosity, can bring you down or lift you up.

DUELING CONSEQUENCES

ENDING A

The next morning the grains gapped limit up on the open. The predetermined limit had been reached, and no more buying could occur that day unless the market came off the limit. It was a dream treat. He'd never felt more sure of himself. This was going to be the big one after all. He decided to take the day off and go surfing. It was a great day. Fairly decent waves and sunlight dancing on the water.

When he got back, he checked the markets. They were closed. He didn't like the day's action. It'd come off the limit up, and had, in fact closed down on the day. He felt an uneasiness creeping over him. They're not going to spook me out, he thought. No way. And then he began to wonder if he was just whistling past the cemetery.

In the morning the grains gapped limit down. Now he was stuck with a MASSIVE position. Shall I buy puts to protect myself from further down-side? he queried. He looked at the rip-off premiums on the puts and decided against it. It'll turn around, he told himself. But it didn't.

The next five days were limit down. Greg researched conditions in the Middle West. The crops weren't in any better shape than they'd been before. It's got to turn around he thought.

Every night Greg slept in fits and starts. He relived all the losses he'd ever had, and he dreamt of losses he'd never had. Sometimes in his dreams he couldn't see the numbers on the screen. Other times his computer would go down, and he'd try to make a phone call to his broker but he couldn't remember the phone number or even his account number.

The markets lifted on the seventh day. Greg unwound his entire position as quickly as he could. All in all he'd lost a half million dollars on the trade. But he was still in business.

He vaguely remembered a story that the hypnotist Milton Ericson had told his patients. It went something like this.

When Milton was a young boy, he and his brothers had grown wheat. They'd gone with their father to look at the wheat.

"Boys," the father had said, "this is no ordinary crop. This is a bumper crop."

They walked home thinking about the money and reveling in their good fortune. The next day it rained all day. And the next day. And the next day. And the next day.

When the rain stopped, they revisited the field. All the wheat had been beaten into the ground.

Their father said, "Let's hope we can get enough seed out of it, and next year we'll plant again and look forward to a crop we can harvest."

Greg looked forward to his next opportunity to plant and harvest. This time he'd keep his positions within size. Above all, he'd watch out for the stories he might tell himself.

ENDING B

The next morning the market gapped limit up. Just as he'd expected. The trade was going his way. Add again if it comes off limit? Nah. Never. That would be a fool's option. He didn't intend to live in a fool's paradise. He began to feel uneasy. The markets will do whatever they have to do to give the most people the most pain, he remembered.

His apprehensive feeling got stronger. Without any more thought he began selling out his position. He took it off slowly and steadily pausing every so often so as not to rattle the market. It came off the limit. He continued his selling. He got the last of his position off just before it got to even.

Greg had seen this kind of action before. As the markets started going negative, he began selling short. He kept his position size normal. No more outsize trading, he thought. He put in a GTC (good til cancelled) buy stop a little above even. Then he went surfing.

SURFING

Greg hung out in the water with his surf board waiting for the next big wave. It was a glorious day with the surface of the water reflecting all the glories of the sun. Fire and water, he thought, blending on the surface. Who knows what was under the surface—smooth sand or razor sharp coral, harmless fish or man eating sharks?

He often thought of surfing as a perfect metaphor for trading. You partner with the forces you're given. You wait patiently for the big wave rather than chase the small ones and miss the big one. Greg halfway believed in the ninth wave theory—that the ninth wave would surge and carry you all the way to shore. When you catch that wave, you ride it to the end.

While surfing was exciting and fun, it was also dangerous. Just like trading. You can trade or surf successfully for years, and then one day your number is up. Greg thought of Mark Foo, the champion surfer, who was killed surfing. He thought of all the guys who have the courage to stand in front of twenty foot waves because they think they can make it.

Like life itself, he thought. You live it with optimism and courage and wring/ring the most out of it. Or you live it with timidity and narrow vision, pruning your dreams until nothing much happens. Either way you die in the end. You might as well live it fully, enjoying all that's there, or you're just putting in time, he decided.

He thought about randomness. Anything can happen, good or bad, in trading or in life. You meet the partner of your dreams, or your trading makes you rich over night. Your mate suddenly leaves you for a younger person, or a rare event wipes out your trading capital.

It was like the black swan problem. You just can't know that because all the swans you've seen are white that there are no black swans; but when you've seen a black swan, then you know that all swans are not white. You just don't know, he thought.

49

HOW GREED DISTORTS PERCEPTION

I wrote the two endings not to be glib and facile. I wrote the two endings because every time we enter or exit a market, we have two possibilities at least. If greed overcomes us, whether it be greed born of scarcity or greed engendered by grandiosity, we'll lose touch with our past experience and with current reality. Greed has a way of distorting perceptions. We do not see things as they are but as we are. A greedy person sees things through greedy eyes.

Greed encourages us to concoct stories. And the stories we tell ourselves may be motivating but they may also be misleading. When you find yourself telling yourself a story, be wary. Is it your imagination or is it based on facts so far revealed. Stories are powerful. And wonderful. But when you're trading, you have to stick with reality as known, and move forward with calculated probabilities. Sometimes things are just too good to be true, or just too good to last.

Sometimes greed causes an urgency that causes you to act and react too quickly. The fear of missing out or the fear of leaving money on the table (another form of missing out), generates a hurried generalizing that moves away from perceivable facts.

You rush before the trade matures, or you act without analysis. If you feel a sense of hurry, be alerted. Good trading can be quick, but it isn't rushed. Ask yourself, what are the probabilities now?

THE ISSUE OF THE RANDOM EVENT

"Alas, investors and businesses are not paid in probabilities, they are paid in dollars. Accordingly, it is not how likely an event is to happen that matters, it is how much is made when it happens that should be the consideration. How frequent the profit is irrelevant, it is the magnitude of the outcome that counts."
—Nasim Taleb

The problem with being greedy and overtrading even when the probabilities are very high is that anything can happen and catch you off guard. In Greg's case, it wasn't really a random event that changed the direction of the market. Weather markets are known to rapidly shift, sometimes even without a genuine change in the weather or a probable alteration of supply and demand. But surprise random events can and do occur, and you need to keep this in your calculation while you trade.

You can have all the probabilities in the world lined up in your favor, and then one giant random event can occur and change the consequences. In trading this is often referred to a possibility of ruination. Savvy traders are always on the alert for that random event that can bring them down.

In the alternative you could have a random event suddenly occur that will bring you a windfall. For example, you're long a large amount of calls on a stock, and overnight that company is taken over. You go to bed with modest wealth, and you wake up rich.

The reverse would have happened to you if—even with the probabilities in your favor—you were short a large amount of those same calls. You go to be with modest wealth, and you wake up broke.

The possibility of a surprise random event tells us that we cannot over trade. No matter the probabilities, no matter the desire to become rich quickly, we simply cannot allow greed to lead us into putting on a position that is out of alignment with our total trading capital.

AN ANTIDOTE TO GREED

Think in terms of abundance. Be aware and appreciative of the plenty that is surrounding you, even as you anticipate more to come.

Look for all the riches you already have in your life. Rejoice in those possessions you have now. Pay attention to the wealth of people and friendships that exist for you. Be grateful for your trading and other money making skills. Affirm your myriad abilities. Notice how your learning keeps increasing. Be aware of your health. Attend to what Carl Sandburg called the "paydays of lilacs and sunsets".

Above all, observe the opportunities past, present, and future in your life and in your trading. There are so many opportunities that it's really about identifying and selecting those opportunities that you could best utilize. Look forward to those opportunities yet to come, and know that you will be able to see them and take full advantage of them. When you do this, there will be no need to over emphasize the current opportunity. This is just one of many chances to make money.

Notice the wealth of others. Bless it. Whenever you see affluence and abundance, affirm it. There is no room in your heart for resentment or envy, because one day such riches can be yours. Remember your prosperity starts with your ideas.

YOUR PLACE IN THE UNIVERSE

Maintain your connection with the vastness of the universe. Be humble in the presence of all the beauty and greatness around you. As you do this the tendency to be grandiose will fade, and you will still realize that you can participate fully in the abundance of the universe. As you do this you develop a healthy contentment mixed with a healthy desire to trade appropriately for your account.

TAKING INVENTORY AND ADJUSTING

1. Make a list of the trading actions you take that could be a manifestation of greed.

2. List the actions you would rather take.

3. Name the emotion you would need to feel in order to take these actions consistently.

4. Write down the beliefs you would need to hold in order to feel and act the way you choose.

5. Write these beliefs into well formulated affirmations. An affirmation needs to be stated positively in the present as if it were already true. An affirmation is a statement made in the present about the future as if it had already occurred in the past.

6. Let these affirmations become a part of you. Write them on cards, repeat them, record them, listen to them, incant them, and let them become a natural part of your way of thinking and doing and feeling.

7. Make a mental image of the affirmation already realized.

8. Believe the certainty of your achievement.

SUPPORTIVE BELIEFS

- I can always make enough money to meet my needs and wants.

- There will be time to learn and develop and create.

- I am enough. I have enough. I can create enough.

- The universe is abundant.

- Life and the markets provide me with rich and recurring opportunities.

Chapter 3

OVERCOMING THE SIN OF RECKLESSNESS

*"Money becomes unimportant. What matters is success.
The sensible thing would be for me to stop,
but I can't. I have to keep aiming higher and
higher—just for the thrill."*
—Aristotle Onasis

To trade effectively you need to be a risk taker—to have the courage, and maybe even enjoy, placing your capital at risk. But there's a world of difference between taking a risk of the appropriate size with the probabilities clearly in mind and just taking a risk for the sake of it. Risk taking is an essential ingredient of trading, but unnecessary risk taking is not.

Reckless traders haven't weighed the odds. Frequently they trade just for the fun of trading. They have the attitude of "Let's just get in and see what happens." Often they'll trade just for the thrill of it. Some will even trade in larger and larger size just to keep it interesting.

The trouble with being reckless in any area of your life is that you endanger yourself and others. Life is filled with enough unknowns and surprise disasters without adding to them. Your lover dies or leaves you. Hurricanes and tornadoes crash through towns. The guy behind you on the freeway stops paying attention and crashes into you. A crazed man in the subway pushes a waiting woman into the path of an oncoming train. A disgruntled client or neighbor decides to sue you. Any given day you can turn on the radio or television or pick up a newspaper or magazine and find out more such things happening or about to happen. Just thinking about the possibility of such occurrences can put a normal person into a state of anxiety.

For some, the willingness to indulge in wild behavior relieves the sense of something awful about to happen. Recklessness enters into the equation and erases anxiety. Live and let live. Stride right into life. Play in the market. Swim way out into the ocean. Kiss your neighbor's wife or husband. Go ahead and do it and see what happens. You only live once. It's only money, or health, or reputation.

The attitude of recklessness gives a sense of freedom and of adventure. Live life to the hilt! Turn down an empty cup. Love and lose, but don't not love. Bet your bottom dollar.

"His passions make man live, his wisdom merely makes him last."
—Chamfort

We want and need to stay in the game of life and trading for a good long time. While we can't cower, we can't crash right in either. We need thoughtful balance.

Recklessness is acting without reckoning. A person acts without thought to the consequences. When we reckon, we calculate the expectancies. We understand that there will be a settling of the results, and we take that into account before we act.

When Confucius was asked who he would take to war, he replied that he would not want somebody who did not care if he lived or died. He would rather have somebody who believed he could succeed by strategy. He affirmed that strategy, not recklessness, is what is needed.

SECOND MURDERER: *"I am one, my liege,*
"Whom the vile blows and buffets of the world
Have so incens'd, that I am reckless what
I do to spite the world."

FIRST MURDERER: *"I another,*
So weary with disasters, tugg'ed with fortune,
That I would set my life on any chance,
To mend it or be rid on't."
—William Shakespeare

Having nothing more to lose does not put a person into a better position to win: it simply means that losing has lost its significance. Winning is another issue. A trader who comes to the point where he doesn't care anymore is in deep trouble. One reckless act can follow another. Nicholas Leeson who brought down the Barings Bank with his reckless trading is a good example of such heedlessness. The Barings Bank had been in business for centuries; indeed, this was the bank that lent the United States the money to make the Louisiana purchase. One trader demolished the bank in a short period of time with his dreadfully reckless trading.

EXCITEMENT SEEKING

For many people life is a quest for excitement. In an effort to avoid boredom or to simply gain a sense of truly being alive, excitement seekers may indulge in a variety of activities, legal or illegal. Trading, gambling, hazardous sports, and wild parties are legal. Robbing banks, shop lifting, wilding, and speeding on throughways are illegal.

Trading and gambling involve financial risk. Certain sports and careless driving involve physical risk. Excitement can be found in either kind of risk. Examples of physical excitement would be bungee jumping, bull fighting, race car driving, surfing, mountain climbing, and so forth. People take their sport to the edge of their ability in order to feel exhilaration. As a well know British sports parachutist put it:

"I know that the risk sharpens things up, makes you more aware. You have an increased perception of things…You know…how green the bloody grass is…If you haven't been there, you can never quite understand, and if you have been there, you can never quite explain."
—Shea-Simmonds

Or as a race car driver of the fifties put it:

"You go through a corner absolutely flat out, right on the ragged edge, but absolutely in control, on your own line to an inch, the car just hanging there, the tires as good as geared to the road, locked to it, and yet you know that if you ask one more mile an hour of the car, if you put another five pounds of sidethrust on it, you'll lose the whole flaming vehicle as surely as if someone has smeared the road with grease. So you stay just this side of that fraction of extra weight that could ruin everything and perhaps kill you to boot, and you are on top of it all, and the exhilaration, the thrill is tremendous."
—Stirling Moss

Many of my trading clients involve themselves with what I would consider dangerous sports. They love the challenge. They love the danger. They love the charge they get from participating in these sports. But they don't exceed their skill levels. They are risk takers and risk managers, not risky adventurers.

Other trading clients look to gambling for excitement on the weekends. They like the thrill of financial risk. Once again, they are careful odds players; and they don't exceed the odds. They take it to the edge, but not over. The problem gambler, on the other hand, needs gambling to feel alive; and will often prefer losing to boredom.

Trading, as gambling, can be misused to create a sense of intensity and aliveness. Some traders trade for the primary purpose of creating excitement in their lives. Most of these traders will indeed produce excitement, but it is doubtful that they will produce consistent profits. The need to take a chance can supercede the need to wait patiently for an appropriate setup. The idea of let's get in and see what happens will produce a happening, but there is no probability of profit there.

EXCITEMENT AND ANXIETY

Some people are primarily excitement seekers while others are generally anxiety avoiders. Others do both. Seeking excitement is not the same as experiencing excitement. Nor is avoiding anxiety the same as being anxious.

At the other extreme of excitement is boredom, and at the other polarity of anxiety is relaxation. Excitement can turn into anxiety and back and forth again depending on the perceived danger. Similarly relaxation and boredom can shift back and forth in response to the interest level.

In a single trade or a single trading day a person can experience all four of these emotions—anxiety, excitement, relaxation, and boredom. The physiology of excitement and anxiety are the same. The physiology of relaxation and boredom are also similar, although boredom is a bit more listless.

The experience of each of these emotions is, however, vastly different. Anxiety and boredom are negative, and excitement and relaxation are positive. Anxiety and excitement are high arousal emotions while relaxation and boredom are low arousal emotions.

Most traders are in a state of high arousal when they trade. How traders interpret the experience of trading will determine whether excitement or anxiety is the dominant emotion. Those who are experiencing excitement are thinking about the 65% probability of profits that their methods offer them. Those who are feeling anxiety are focused on the 35% possibility of loss. What are your dominant emotions when you trade or even think about trading? Looking at your life in general, do you look for exciting activities or do you look for the safest course to take?

Michael J. Apter has written a fascinating book on the importance of excitement seeking to certain people as well as to society as a whole. The book is entitled *The Dangerous Edge: The Psychology of Excitement.*[1]

PROTECTIVE FRAMES

According to Mr. Apter, to turn a high arousal experience into excitement rather than anxiety, you need to have a protective frame in place. One type of protective frame would be having confidence in your ability to handle a situation. Another would be to perceive yourself as being in a safety-zone where you would not be vulnerable to injury. Still another way to develop a protective frame would be to develop a sense of detachment.

CONFIDENCE

With confidence the individual feels assured that she will skillfully avoid trauma in spite of the realization of the presence of danger. A trader can trust her methods and rely on the probabilities. She can trust herself to apply her methods in a timely fashion with discipline. She believes that the trade will go her way, and if it does not, she can exit gracefully. Thus, the confidence in her methods and herself produces a protective frame that allows her to feel exhilaration rather than fear as she trades.

SAFETY-ZONE

A person who perceives himself to be in a safety-zone feels that he is in no immediate danger, nor any possibility of slipping into danger. The trader with his money in T Bills or short term corporate bonds could perceive himself to be in a safety-zone (despite the fact that a bank or brokerage firm could go bankrupt and the government fail to insure the money). A more adventurous trader could believe himself to be in a safety-zone as long as he has placed his protective stop loss orders in the market. Or another trader could perceive himself in a safety-zone because he has not placed all his money at risk.

DETACHMENT

Detachment provides a distance from the danger and so works as a protective frame. You can step outside yourself and observe the trade from the point of view of a neutral observer. Asking questions helps. What would I think if I weren't in this trade? Or you could look at the trade from the point of view of a coach or mentor. What would guru so and so think about this trade?

One way to gain detachment is through practicing mental rehearsal. The trade isn't real—it's only imaginary and so it's easy to feel protected. As you do the mental rehearsal, you develop good trading habits. It's easy to be disciplined when there's no money on the line. Also, as you repeat the mental rehearsal, you develop what I call emotional inoculation. You get used to the tensions of trading, and it's not so scary when you're actually doing it. A little of the thing that scares you toughens you up to accept more of what before had overwhelmed you.

You can also create a healthy distance from your trading by trading very, very small. You begin with baby steps, and when you get steady on your feet and can trade consistently, you slowly add more size.

Paper trading or virtual or simulated trading can also provide detachment. I am often asked what I think of simulated trading. My answer is that this kind of trading is a good way to test out whether or not a method works in forward time. It's also a good way to train yourself to become adept at applying that method. However, it does have a serious drawback. People who paper trade too long, get too comfortable simply doing this. They procrastinate starting the real thing, and when they do finally start, they may find themselves incapable or unwilling to risk real capital. They have unwittingly developed a hobby that they enjoy, but they do not have a business or profession.

Taking the long view of your trading is another way that can assist you in detaching from any given trade or trading day. Look at each trade as but one in a series of many trades. Each trade is but one in a clump of trades. Each trade or each trading day becomes statistically insignificant. It's just like one rainy or sunny day. One trade or one trading day is not the prototype for the rest of your trading life. Therefore you can't allow yourself to become too elated or too dejected. Remember this too shall pass.

GAMBLING AS RECKLESSNESS

It is common knowledge that 9 out of 10 futures traders lose money. How can this be when futures trading is a zero sum game: half the people are short and half are long? You would expect half the people to win at least half of the time. But it doesn't seem to be so. There seems to be something wrong with the way the mind assesses risk and opportunity. And so the majority of futures traders gamble, and find out too late that their approach simply didn't work. They were misled, or they miscalculated.

Let's take a look at gaming as gambling is called within that profession. It's a big business in the United States. According to the General Accounting Office, $54 billion is spent on gambling, and that's more than all other recreational spending put together. It's replaced baseball as the national pastime. Whereas 70 million people go to major league baseball games, 107 million people visit casinos in Las Vegas, Atlantic City, and Mississippi alone.

The worst odds of all gambling is offered by the lotteries in 37 states. The state pays out 50 cents on the dollar on lottery tickets, so you've lost 50 cents the moment you buy the ticket. Then the odds of winning are atrocious, but humans have a hard time perceiving and calculating very long odds. The Powerball lottery odds are something like 80.1 million to 1.

We don't comprehend the odds. One way to grasp the high improbability of wining is making the odds concrete rather than merely mathematical. To have a reasonable chance of winning the Massachusetts lottery, you would have to buy a lottery ticket each week for 1.6 million years. If you drive 10 miles to buy a Powerball ticket, you are 16 times more likely to die in a car accident on the way there than you are to win.

Long shots do happen. People do win, and we see them on television and in the newspapers. Their winning becomes very real and substantial to us. All the millions and millions of losers don't enter our consciousness. Gamblers thrive on the illusion of control. They pick the numbers. They buy the ticket. They roll the dice. They chose the red or the black. Gamblers look at their wins as manifestation of their skill and intuition. They look at their losses as a near miss or a fluke. They just don't comprehend the odds, and they don't grasp that their winning or losing is quite out of their control.

In order to not be reckless—to not be gambling with our trading—we need to calculate the odds rigorously. We need to look risk squarely in the eyes. We need to beware our illusory dreams.

A RECKLESS TRADER

He knew he wasn't going to live 700 years. This was the time to get it done. This was the time to live. Jason raced his Ferrari down the highway on his way to work. He was a floor trader at the CBOT.

He looked forward to the day's trading. Today whenever he could find an edge, he'd step up the size. This was no time to be meek. There was that house on Lake Michigan that he wanted to buy. Maybe he could get it over the weekend. Pay cash and own it outright.

He felt so lucky to be going to work. His work was just like a big game. The game was a daring adventure. He'd be aggressive and risk seeking with his winners. He'd add to them. He'd also be aggressive in unloading his losers. He knew that people on their deathbeds don't have regret for the things they've done, but they have remorse and sadness for those things they never did. He was going to do it all.

News was coming out at 9:00. He was pretty sure he knew which way it was going to go and how the crowd would react to it. He'd position himself big before the numbers and then add to it when it went his way. He knew it was a dangerous thing to do, but you didn't get anywhere playing it safe. Besides it would be a really great adrenaline fix.

When the news came out, Jason found himself on the wrong side of the market. He couldn't find a bid. Aggressive as he was, he couldn't sell his position. It was racing against him and he couldn't unload. By the time things settled down and he was finally flat, he was down a bundle.

"Why did I bet the news? Why do I get so arrogant? What if I blow out? Really blow out all the way?"

"Oh well, I'll make it back on the number this afternoon. Lightning doesn't strike twice in the same place."

RECKLESSNESS TAKES MANY FORMS

Maybe Jason will, and maybe he won't make the money back on the next trade. Sooner or later, though, with an all-out-go-for-it-big-no-matter-what attitude, he will realize his fear. He will, as he put it, blow out.

Recklessness takes many forms. Recklessness is not only adventuring. Jason's over-trading in terms of size and frequency and gambling on events is just one form of recklessness. There are many others.

Strangely enough, the buy and hold strategy urged by so called conservative advisors and money managers is also hugely dangerous. Witness those who held unto "good" stocks throughout the 2000-2002 (and at the current writing 2003) bear market. They squandered their money away without even realizing they were gambling.

Laziness is another form of recklessness. The trader, who starts trading with insufficient preparation, heedlessly endangers his money. Perhaps he hasn't bothered to find out what works in trading. He just starts trading from the seat of his pants. Or he takes what somebody else claims works and trades it without verification. Fortunes have been lost buying and trading systems that in the long run don't work out.

Equally reckless is the timid person, who having developed an effective trading method, cannot or does not consistently follow the entry and exit signals. It is foolhardy to wait for confirmation that a signal will go your way and enter the trade late. It is also dangerous to unequally trade a system by picking and choosing entries and exits. The system was based on probabilities, and you cannot safely unequally apply them.

I frequently encounter traders who have spent months and sometimes years preparing a system to trade, and expect to trade it without a minute's work of preparation on themselves and their inner psychological tendencies. All their attention has been painstakingly and lavishly spent on exterior trading methods with no thought at all for the interior process of trading. Without doing change work on themselves, they are unable to benefit from their long research. Even if they don't lose money by not trading their methods, they are foolishly throwing away their opportunity to make future profits, and they are wasting their past efforts.

Trading without awareness of the randomness of the unfolding of events is also reckless. One random event can undo the most carefully constructed trading plans. The undoing of Long Term Capital is an example of this.

Long Term Capital had two nobel laureates and some very successful traders who had developed a trading system that had a very small chance of losing. Unfortunately, when they were massively over positioned in an interest rate spread, a random situation occurred, and they almost brought down the financial and banking sector. They were so arrogantly sure of their methods that they overlooked the possibility of a single random occurrence. Because their trade was so big and the ramifications so broad, the Fed arranged a bailout.

It is a normal human tendency not to be aware of the random quality of life. We like to think that everything has been laid out in orderly patterns and the future will mirror the past. Often it does. However, it is careless not to be prepared for the random happening that can bring your trading to tatters and you to your knees. That is why you never trade too large for your account to weather a random event. Remember if you are right 99% of the time, but you bet 100% of your funds, you will lose it all on the 1% when you are mistaken.

SOME CONSIDERATIONS OF YOUR RECKLESSNESS

1. When was the last time you traded recklessly?

2. Were there other times?

3. What lessons did you learn?

4. Was there ever a time when you were too cautious or timid—when you did not have enough of a sense of adventure and ended up being reckless?

5. How would you like to behave in the future?

6. What attitude would help you behave without either timid or aggressive recklessness?

7. What resources do you already have that will help you entertain this helpful attitude?

8. Use them.

SUPPORTIVE BELIEFS

- Anything can happen, so I always trade in moderation, in the appropriate size.

- Anything can happen, so I always use protective stop loss orders.

- I have all the courage I need to trade my proven methodology.

- I know that I am central to the results of my trading, so I prepare my conscious and unconscious mind to trade effectively.

- I trade with probabilities foremost in my mind.

- I verify that my trading guidelines put the probabilities in my favor.

- I have all the time I need to create my wealth.

[1] *The Dangerous Edge: The Psychology of Excitement,* Michael J. Apter, The Free Press, a Division of Macmillan, Inc., 1992, ISBN 0-02-900765-8.

Chapter 4

OVERCOMING THE SIN OF PERFECTIONISM

*"True perfection is achieved only by those
who are prepared to destroy it."*
—Sir Kenneth Clark

Trading is not, and never has been, a game of perfect. Trading is, and only can be, a game of probabilities. Probability, not perfection, is the base upon which you build your trading plan. Probability, not perfection, is the platform on which you execute your plan. As a trader you are a pragmatist, not a perfectionist

It has been my observation that maybe one-ninth of traders, despite knowing that all we have are probabilities, still seek to improve the odds to something as close to 100% as they can get. They may not come right out and admit it, but they hold themselves to some impossible standard of performance. Such high standards not only decrease their comfort, they decrease their profitability. And therein lies the irony. Seeking to do better, they do worse.

*"Finality is death. Perfection is finality. Nothing is
perfect. There are lumps in it."*
—James Stephens

JEROME

Jerome set out to design himself as perfect a trading system as he could. He read, he studied, he took courses, he back tested, he combined systems, he added filters and more filters. With each new addition, he seemed to improve the performance. Finally, after two and one-half years, he had what he considered to be the optimal trading system. Unwittingly, and without ever intending to do so, Jerome curve fitted his system to the past. While past is said to be prologue to the future, when it comes to optimized trading systems, it's nothing but backwards wishful thinking. In real time Jerome's system simply didn't work.

FRED

After three years of preparation in designing a currency trading methodology, Fred was ready to put it to work. At first he began by paper trading. Even the simulated trading made him tense. With each new signal he felt a sense of foreboding. He felt like something awful would happen if the paper trade lost money. Surprisingly, and maybe not so surprisingly, the paper track record was very good. Fred's long and pain staking work had paid off. He had created a robust and viable method. Strangely enough, the better the method worked, the more tense Fred became. He dreaded—even on paper—a possible drawdown. Instead of feeling gratification, Fred was feeling a sense of muffled doom which so far has never come. Of course, the doom cannot arrive as long as Fred remains paper trading. Neither will the rewards or profitability develop as long as he continues only trading on paper.

PATTY

Patty had been taught how to trade by a veteran trader. For one year an older trader had mentored her. He openly and generously coached her in his effective trading strategies. "Time to begin, Patty," he had told her. And she knew it was time. She knew what to do, and just how to do it. Furthermore, she wanted to please her mentor. The problem was she just couldn't get started. Whenever she saw a trade, she sat there frozen. She was terrified of making a mistake, and so she did nothing. As the proverb goes, if you don't make mistakes, you don't make anything. Patty made no mistakes, no money, and no progress.

AN IMPOSSIBLE TASK

"Whoever thinks a faultless piece to see
Thinks what ne'er was, nor is, nor
e'er shall be."
—Alexander Pope

My sister, Marion Barrons, says, "Perfectionists are always striving and never arriving. They are never able to be where they are because they're always trying to be better. They put terrible consequences on themselves to get where they think they should go. Even when they get there, they don't know it, because they're always looking for flaws to eliminate. If they don't find any flaws, they still search. They are damned if they do and damned if they don't."

Certainly neither Jerome nor Carl nor Patty arrived where they sought to go. They went part of the way, but they couldn't get all the way home. Perfectionism took them some distance, but they couldn't arrive at their ultimate goal of trading profitably. The desire to achieve perfectly got them started only to become their insurmountable obstacle to success. Successful trading has nothing to do with being perfect.

APPROXIMATIONS NOT EXACTITUDE

"One of the great evils of trading is false
exactness…Trading is a fuzzy process and I mean fuzzy
in the best sense of the word. That is, as in fuzzy logic, as
in the willingness to accept the idea that things aren't
exactly quantifiable and to forge ahead anyway."
—John Bollinger

Patterns don't repeat exactly. You have to allow for some deviation. When you wait for patterns to line up exactly, you miss a lot of good trades. You need to allow for the patina that comes through time, the slight distortions that probably will work out anyway.

For example, if you wait for your target projection to hit exactly on the number, you may miss by a sliver, and then where will you be? You'll be watching your profits deteriorate. You need to beware a false precision which is simply not available in the rough and tumble trading arena.

THE ORIGINS OF PERFECTIONISM

"And where did you get the idea of how much less than magnificent you are? From the only people whose word you would take on everything. From your mother and your father."
—Neale Donald Walsch

The perfectionist doesn't come into this world with the mission of being perfect. No. We are born as human beings with the ability to unfold and develop in accordance with our nature and our experience. Some children, unfortunately, get the message early on that they have an obligation to be perfect.

Remember in school when you listened to the teacher ridicule another student for giving the wrong answer? Remember how you waved your hand when you were sure you knew the answer, but how you shrank down hoping not to be noticed when you didn't know? Recall how you would study for tests trying so hard to prepare all the correct answers to the questions you knew and didn't know would be asked?

Education too frequently engenders the belief that there is a right answer and a wrong answer, and you'd better get it right. 100 % is what you're expected to deliver in order to get the A. And some of us were flat out expected to get A's.

There is a tendency these days for parents to be expected to get involved with a child's homework. In taking on this task, they often develop a conflict with the reluctant student to deliver fully completed and fully accurate homework—in other words, "perfect" preparation. The child may acquire a sense that there's only one right way of doing things.

Such approaches to education can develop in some a compulsion to live up to the highest standards, and with that an uncomfortable state of anxiety. Others may develop avoidance techniques such as laziness or disinterest. Rarely does this kind of an approach develop a state of joyful curiosity and exploration.

I believe—and this is just my opinion and perhaps not relevant here—that young students should be given clear instructions by the teacher before taking their homework home. If additional explanation is needed, they should have it in the form of books or explanatory sheets or suggested places to go get information. The role of the parents then becomes one of providing a conducive environment for study, clear expectations, and warm encouragement. The homework and the responsibility are the child's. There is no need to create a joint project or an unfortunate tussle or battle of wills. The child learns self-reliance and self-confidence by doing it himself.

Apart from schooling issues, perfectionism is frequently engendered by home and family conditions. Perfectionists start out as good little boys and girls. Often they are given extraordinary responsibilities—perhaps taking care of siblings or even a parent. The responsibilities heaped on their young shoulders are often those of an adult.

They develop a heavy sense of seriousness and the need to act like an adult. Sometimes they feel as if they have to justify their very existence. Just being a child is somehow not enough.

INTERNAL CRITIC

Parental harsh criticism is often a formative part of perfectionism. In order to avoid painful criticism, children begin to monitor themselves excessively in order to avoid blunders. In so doing, they develop an exacting internal critical voice. This voice becomes a dominating part of their thoughts. It never occurs to them that this voice might be wrong. The critical chatter severely limits their ability to just try things out and see what happens.

ANGER

There's something basically unfair about having to do things perfectly to somebody else's standards or those same standards which have been internalized as one's own. Such exacting standards can create great frustration and anger.

Furthermore, because perfectionists hold themselves to exceptionally high standards, they naturally expect others to live by their code. Remember, they think it's the only and correct code. When others don't live up to their standards, perfectionists may feel the need to make up for the misdeeds, mistakes, or carelessness of others. Of course, this quite easily overburdens them.

The result is quite naturally a seemingly justifiable anger. However, since the expression of anger is often forbidden by their internal code, perfectionists may repress the anger or may simply seethe within.

THE FEAR

The basic fear of perfectionists is of coming up short—of being wrong, inferior, bad, defective, or simply not good enough. Their basic desire is to be good, virtuous, accurate, and correct. Thus, they come away with the internal message that they are good or okay if they do what is right. But how do you know what is right in trading?

RIGHT AND WRONG

"All great discoveries have been made from a willingness, and ability, to not be right."
—Neale Donald Walsch

The first thing a trader with a perfectionist bent needs to grasp is that there is no right or wrong way to trade. True, there are winning and losing trades, and these are to be expected and accepted as they come along because they cannot be determined in advance. How could somebody hold themselves to the impossible standard of choosing only winning trades?

There are winning and losing methods. Here the idea is to research and choose the best for you of the winning methods you find. Then you hold yourself to the standard of rigorously and consistently applying your chosen method to the market. Being right becomes taking all the trades your system offers you, not taking all the *winning* trades your system offers you.

THE BEST YOU CAN DO

"All you can do is all you can do but all you can do is enough!"
—A. L. Williams

As a trader, you need to keep in mind that all you can do is all you can do. You can't do anymore than what you can do. Your best is your best at the time. Sure, you can back trade—the I should have bought it here and I should have sold it there kind of nonsense. Give yourself a break. You did the best you could at the time. Now the future—ah, that's another thing.

When you identify what trading methods are effective, confirm that they do indeed work profitably, prepare fully, and execute your methods consistently, you have done all you can do for now. You have done the best you can do, and that is enough for now. Let yourself off the hook. Maybe tomorrow or next week or next month you can do better, but accept your results—and yourself—for now.

SELF-ACCEPTANCE

"The curious paradox is that when I accept myself just as I am, I can change."
—Carl Rogers

Perfectionists often feel that if they accept themselves as they are, they have let down their standards, and will fall into an unacceptable mediocrity or worse. But it just doesn't work that way. The more you hold yourself or your behavior as unacceptable, the harder it is to alter your behavior and to restyle yourself. You can get caught up in the thing you don't like and get stuck there.

A powerful affirmation is: "I TOTALLY AND UNCONDITIONALLY ACCEPT MYSELF EVEN THOUGH I HAVE THIS PROBLEM." That doesn't mean you like the problem or plan to keep it. It means you accept yourself even with the problem. Problems are puzzles seeking solutions. When you have defined the problem, you are on your way to the solution.

Resistance hardens the problem. Acceptance softens it. Anyway, you're not accepting the problem: you're accepting yourself. In accepting yourself, you make way for the solution to the difficulty.

Think of a time you accepted something. Maybe it was a gift, a great meal, a sunset, a beautiful day. Relive the experience seeing what you saw, hearing what you heard, and feeling what you felt. Now, just give that same appreciative acceptance to yourself. Notice what that feels like, listen to how you language your acceptance, and see what it looks like when you accept yourself without reservation.

SELF-APPRECIATION ENGENDERS SELF-ESTEEM

Perfectionist traders often go around looking to see what they're doing wrong, so they can fix it. This is ameliorative to be sure, but look where the focus is. The focus is on the weakness rather than the strength. When you concentrate on your flaws, you begin to feel flawed. Without ever intending to do it, you are whittling away your self-esteem.

I frequently give the assignment to traders to make a list of everything they appreciate about themselves and to keep adding to the list during the course of a week. I also suggest that they ask themselves at the end of the day what they did that day that they're proud of. I tell them to catch themselves doing something right while they're trading and to praise themselves for it at the moment. That way they'll get more of that behavior.

Remember a time when you really appreciated someone or something. It might be an act of kindness or a piece of music or a painting. Relive that experience fully. Now just give that same appreciation to yourself. Observe what it's like to appreciate yourself, listen to what you say to yourself, and allow yourself to feel it.

Now remember a time when you truly esteemed someone—perhaps a teacher, a parent, a friend, a famous person. Re-experience that time noticing what you see and hear and feel. Now give yourself that same esteem. Pay attention how that feels, what it looks like, and how it sounds.

Plan to do this everyday for the next week, every week for the next month, and every month for the next year. The more you accept, appreciate, and esteem yourself, the easier it will get. And soon it will become a habitual attitude, or as I call it in my last book, a habitude.

Perfectionists are reluctant to do this because they think they don't deserve it. Or they're afraid that if they affirm themselves, they'll cease improving. Try it anyway. You can still be realistic even as you build yourself up. I've never met a trader with too much self-esteem. I've met arrogant and egotistical traders and careless traders who were their own undoing, but I've never met a trader who damaged his trading through self-appreciation or self-esteem.

GIVING UP THE NEED TO CONTROL THE FUTURE

It's simply not true that we don't have control over our trading. We decide when to enter. We decide when to exit. We select what markets to trade. We settle on what indicators to utilize. We choose our broker. We determine the what and the when and the how. The only thing we don't have control over is what the market does.

Perfectionist traders tend to want complete control over everything. They have a hard time letting go and just going with the flow. Feeling the need to be in exacting control, they also fret about just how they should go about controlling things. Since everything is up to them, they feel a terrible sense of responsibility.

Often they feel the need to be right. If they equate being right with having only winning trades, they've put an overwhelming burden on themselves, and the minute a trade starts to go against them, they feel out of control. A perfectionist rarely has the attitude of let's get in and see what happens.

> *"Life must be lived forwards, but can only be understood backwards."*
> —Kierkegaard

We can study trading backwards, but we must trade forward, and only then find out what happens. Remember the boilerplate put on all offerings: **PAST RESULTS DO NOT GUARANTEE THE FUTURE PERFORMANCE.** I'll say. The truism is true. We cannot control the future. Maybe we can have some influence, but we do not have dominion over it.

This is hard on certain personality types. No matter how many times they tell themselves to relax and accept what happens, they can't. They think they have to take responsibility for it.

THE IMPORTANCE OF CURIOSITY

One delightful way to approach the future of your trading—or your life for that matter—is to adopt an attitude of curiosity. Curiosity may have killed the cat, but it can save you. What a wonderful way to begin the trading day: "I wonder what will happen today. I wonder if I'll have a really good day." Compare this to: "I hope I make the right decisions. I hope I don't lose money."

When you get curious, lots of avenues open up. Where are the opportunities today? What are the possibilities? What are the probabilities? Where is the next trade? How can I make money today?

You can start with "I wonder how…" And then just state what you want. I wonder how I can become a better trader. I wonder how I can have more fun trading. I wonder how I can improve my results.

Then take that wonderment into the rest of your life. I wonder how I can get a raise. I wonder how I can entice him to fall in love with me. I wonder how I can persuade her to go out with me. I wonder how we can have more fun at home?

An open and optimistic curiosity allows life to unfold in exciting and marvelous ways.

ALTERNATELY FOCUS ON THE BIG PICTURE
AND THE SIGNIFICANT DETAIL

Perfectionists tend to get caught up in detail. This can get in the way of clear minded trading. Much of the detail is unimportant, and simply clutters the mind. Traders with a perfectionist bent would do well to decide in advance what details are significant and what are not.

By altering the focus between big picture and significant detail, a trader can clarify his view of the market and its action.

RECOGNIZING THE GOODNESS WITHIN

There's an old Hindu legend that talks about hiding the divinity within man. According to this legend humankind had misused their divine powers and offended the gods. The gods decided to take away the divine power and hide it someplace that humans would never find it. But where to hide it? If they hid it under the earth, humans would dig down and locate it. If they placed it on the highest mountain, humans would climb up and discover it. If they buried it in the depths of the oceans, mankind would sooner or later find it there.

The gods came up with a plan to utterly hide man's divinity from himself. They decided to hide it deep within each human. They knew that that would be the last place a person would look—within herself.

Your power is within you. Your source of goodness and wisdom and grace and understanding and courage is already within yourself. It's yours for the using. And you can trade with it.

ASSESSING YOUR RELATIONSHIP WITH PERFECTIONISM

1. Do you hold yourself to an unrealistic standard in life or in your trading?

2. Do you feel something terrible will happen if you're not right?

3. Do you feel there's one right way to do things?

4. Do you get inordinately tense about your trading?

5. Do you get angry with yourself for losing?

6. Can you forgive yourself your mistakes?

7. How would you rather respond to the above situations?

8. Practice responding this way. Catch yourself in the middle of the old response, and try the new response.

SUPPORTIVE BELIEFS

- I am perfectly human.

- I do my best and my best is enough.

- I am becoming a better trader.

- Trading is an imperfect art and science.

- The future is not knowable, so I don't have to accurately predict it.

- Being right is following my methods and rules.

- I am worthy of forgiveness.

- I can forgive myself and still improve.

- I pay attention to my progress.

Chapter 5

OVERCOMING THE SIN OF PRIDE

"Tis pride that pulls the country down."
—William Shakespeare

Trading is not about you or me. Trading is about the collective perceptions and reactions of the trading and investing multitudes. It is about time, momentum, price, and volume. It's about ways to observe and measure these things and then to act upon them.

It's not about you. When you assert yourself first and foremost into the equation, you are making a huge mistake. First of all, your attention and energy are being focused on an irrelevancy; i.e., yourself. Second, you distort and delete important information in an effort to preserve or enhance your self image. You need to take yourself out of consideration.

When you put yourself central to any endeavor, you are more likely to create failure than success. In public speaking, for example, it's crucial to keep your mind on the message you're conveying and not on what the audience thinks of you as a speaker. The moment you put your attention on yourself, your communication is badly weakened, and, naturally, the thing you least want occurs. The audience loses respect for you as a speaker. The same is true in sports. Any athlete who focuses on self rather than the task at hand is likely to choke and render a poor performance.

Pride is attaching your ego to the event or situation instead of simply attempting to do your best. When you bring your ego into trading, you lose twofold. You lose your money, and you lose your self esteem.

There are two kinds of pride, each representing one side of the same coin. One side is hubris or arrogance where you feel you could do no wrong. The other side is a puffing up of the self to impress others so they can think highly of you, in order that you can think highly of yourself. One comes from over confidence, the other from a confidence deficit. Both are dangerous.

HUBRIS

"Pride goeth before destruction as a haughty spirit before a fall."
—Proverbs 16:18

Hubris has been defined by the Oxford American Dictionary as "an insolent pride or presumption". The dictionary refers to its use in Greek tragedy as "arrogant pride toward the gods, leading to nemesis." The Oxford English Dictionary defines hubristic as "insolent, contemptuous".

A trader manifests hubris when he thinks he has the deal locked up. He is absolutely sure of his position or his abilities. In such a state of over confidence, he lays himself open to error and reversals.

He might have told himself a story and believed it. He might be so sure of his facts that he doesn't put in a stop. He might be so convinced of his technical analysis that he's tempted to over trade or to add to a losing position. He might have missed his entering signal, but he chases it anyway because he's so sure of the market direction. He may be so certain of his position that he misses the signs that things are changing. His conviction is often not justified, or is no longer justified.

AN ARROGANT TRADER

"There is a fine line between arrogance and self-confidence...Arrogance is a killer."
—Jack Welch

Adam White's equity curve was expanding—exponentially it seemed. He felt more than confident. Somewhere along the line, trading had gotten easy. He really knew what he was doing. He had the touch.

His hedge fund was bulging with money and more money kept poring in. Adam knew there was a limit to what he could handle, so he closed the fund to new investors. Clients were sending in more money, and prospective clients were begging for him to make an exception and take their money anyway. He refused.

He was being written up in financial publications. Adam began to believe what was written about him. He always knew he was a winner, and now he believed he was a super winner. When a friend of his called to discuss the markets, he responded that he didn't have time to discuss that now. He used to spend a lot of time chewing over the markets with his friends. Now he felt he was giving more than he was getting. It was just too time consuming.

Adam and his wife, Mary, decided to take a much needed vacation to an obscure island in the Caribbean—a very exclusive, very private island. They planned to be away for two weeks. The trading was going well, and Adam decided to leave his long and short equity positions in place. He could check the office every day by phone. When they got to the island, Adam discovered that his cell phone didn't work from there. Neither were there land phones that worked. At first it made him quite uneasy. He was out of touch, and nobody in his office had authority to trade the fund. With time, however, he pushed it from his mind. There was something soothing and seductive about an island escape. Two weeks passed quickly and it didn't seem nearly long enough. He allowed Mary to persuade him to stay another week.

When Adam returned to the office, he faced unprecedented losses in the accounts. He had been incommunicado during a crucial shift in the market. The accounts were devastated. I'll make it back, he told himself. He altered and adjusted his positions, but the market reversed again, and now he was facing even greater losses. He was getting whipsawed. Whereas before he could do no wrong, now he could do no right.

Adam considered closing the fund and trading only his own money, but he didn't want to go out with his tail between his legs, looking and feeling like a failure. He'd get a handle on it and find something bold to do to remedy the situation. After all, he told himself, he was Adam White and he could always find a way.

***

If Adam White's bold action doesn't work out, our arrogant trader will find his hubris melting and being replaced by realism or humility. He will be able to trade his way back into the black. He is a good trader and he will ultimately succeed.

Adam will not succeed, however, if he gets trapped in his pride. If he wins and his hubris expands, he will sooner or later face another down fall. If he loses, he may begin desperately to try to prove his worth, to convince himself and others of his ability as a trader. In such a case he will get caught up in the old ego prop.

PRIDE AS EGO PRETENTION

When a trader begins to doubt himself, he may begin urgently to try and prove himself. His trading becomes his gage of self worth. This self-questioning may have its origins in his past or in his trading. Most usually the trader who seeks to establish his value through successful trading has a history of low self worth. He is using the trading as a means to prove his value to himself and to others.

Unfortunately, even if he trades well for a while, the moment he enters a rough patch, he will once again begin to question his self worth. Now he has two problems: SELF ESTEEM AND TRADING RESULTS.

It's dangerous to equate yourself with your trading results. It's even more dangerous to try to prove yourself to yourself through your trading. You might wade in just to prove your bravado. You might refuse to accept a loss because you can't admit to being wrong.

Since trading is simply working with probabilities, and because there are no certainties, it makes no sense to think more highly of yourself if a few probabilities work out, or to feel ashamed if a probability doesn't materialize.

OPTIMISTIC CONFIDENCE, NOT PRIDE, IS WHAT YOU NEED

The arrogant trader has not based his over confidence in reality. He takes short cuts. He trades too large and too frequently. He puffs himself up. He believes his own falsely based legend. In contradistinction, the insecure trader, who is putting on a front for himself or others, really doubts his ability to trade. Neither of these is a truly confident trader. A confident trader is not a proud trader, nor is an optimistic trader a proud trader.

The confident trader knows what to do and how to do it. The optimistic trader expects the trading to be profitable over time. She expects each trade to work out even though she knows there's a possibility of loss. She accepts this because she trusts the larger picture.

Successful traders have a positive self expectancy. They expect to win. And they get what they expect. Two powerful emotions in trading are fear and desire. A losing trader fears loss, and somehow creates that loss. A winning trader desires to win and will win over time, because she will plan for winning and take whatever steps are necessary to win. (Find a winning strategy. Verify that it is profitable historically and in current time. Trade it efficiently and effectively.)

Fear and desire, in the final analysis, are the two driving emotions of our life as well as our trading. They are mirror images of what we want and don't want. One of them dominates our thoughts and our tendencies.

For example, consider your views on physical health. Do you fear sickness? Do you dwell on it? Be careful or you will create it. Do you desire health? Do you move towards health? Do you have healthy, health goals? Do you envision a future blessed with radiant health? Chances are you will create it.

Elvis Presley was preoccupied with the memory of his mother's death of heart disease at age 43. He was fearful that he too would die at age 43 of a heart attack. He died at age 43 of a heart attack.

This is not just happenstance. We move in the direction of our dominant thoughts. What kind of pictures do you have of your future? Health or sickness? Abundance or scarcity? Do you imagine yourself in that legendary ten percent who win at trading or in the alleged ninety percent who lose?

You can change the way you think. Do you fear poverty or lack? Change your thoughts to images of wealth and affluence. Create for yourself a compelling future. Make your goals vivid. Articulate them with strong, clear words. Make pictures of them actually realized. Visualize and state your goals as if they were already accomplished. You will be magnetized to your compelling future.

"Losers let it happen. Winners make it happen."
—Dennis Waitley

Winners are driven by desire. They have a clear image of what they want, and they work consistently toward that success. Losers are tormented by fear. They resist risking failure on the way to success. Once fixated on the thing you fear, you are on your way there. Losers also tend to lose again and again in the same way. Trading is a do it yourself program. It is also a do it to yourself program.

Winners are motivated towards their desire. Our current dominant thoughts impel us in that direction. If we fear, we relive experiences of our past pain and failure. If we desire, we remember times of triumph and joy. Fearful people hear themselves saying: I can't. I have to. I don't want to. I can't afford to lose. People motivated by desire will say: I want to. I can. I will. I choose to win.

THE IMPORTANCE OF A HEALTHY SELF IMAGE

Self image works as a thermostat of our behaviors. If we perform above our self image, unconsciously we will bring ourselves back down to the expected level. If we perform below our self image, we will automatically take action to lift that behavior up to the expected level.

The salesman who sees himself as a $75,000 a year man, will earn that $75,000 whether he is given a difficult territory or an easy territory. He stays within his self image. A trader will do the same thing.

Self image acts like an unconscious self governing device. We have images of ourselves in all areas of our life. I'm a great dancer. I can't cook. I'm a so-so athlete. I'm good with people. I can't sell. I'm no good with numbers. I'm very creative. I'm really good on the phone. I can talk anybody into anything. I have social phobia. I hate going to large parties. I'm a good mother. I'm a great lover. I'm an impatient father. I'm attractive to the opposite sex.

Traders have different images regarding different parts of their trading. I can read the markets. I'm really nimble getting out of a trade. I can always get out of a trade gracefully. I can't take a loss. I get really nervous in a trade. I always jump out of a trade too soon. I can sit through the bumps. I'm only as good as my last trade. I always look forward to the next trade. I trust my intuition. My intuition's always wrong. I'm a good systems trader. I facilitate my model. I can't seem to follow a system. I always think I know better.

"I'll never do *that* again!" we shout. And then we do it again. The lesson doesn't sink in. Could that have to do with the image we hold of ourselves in the market?

Self image has been created, and it can be changed. Your self concept is merely that—an idea. You thought it up, and you can change it. Identity has no reality in the external world. It's not something you can touch or put in a wheel barrow. It has no more reality than any other concept.

You have identified yourself with certain attributes. Others have identified you with certain qualities. When you accept these qualities and attributes, they become your identity. Since it's your identity, you cling to it for better or worse because it is you. The truth is that you can expand and alter your identity. What would the ideal you be like?

Write down a description of the ideal you. Step into that person and see how that feels. How would the ideal you trade? How would the ideal you respond to people? How would the ideal you go about living a life? Ask yourself, if I were already the person/trader I want to be, how would I handle this situation? You can also mentally rehearse behaving this way.

I work with my clients to imagine themselves trading the way they ideally would. They do mental rehearsal repeatedly seeing themselves trading the markets consistently and profitably. I make them self hypnosis tapes that they listen to over and over again. The unconscious mind does not recognize the difference between imaginary and actual experience. The image of themselves as traders shifts, and soon they correct the behaviors that tripped them up.

Sit quietly at the beginning and ending of each trading day and imagine yourself trading your plan. If during the day you stumble, take the time to imagine yourself doing the correct thing. At the end of the day, if you've fouled up, mentally practice trading the day over again, only this time imagine following good trading principles.

PRIDE INTERFERES WITH CLARITY

"Not everything that can be counted counts, and not everything that counts can be counted."
—Albert Einstein

"The first principle is that you must not fool yourself—and you are the easiest person to fool."
—Richard Feynman

If you're busy protecting or inflating your self image, you won't be able to observe the market with clarity. In trading you need to think clearly and to think clearly in probabilities.

And yet it's hard for humans to think in terms of probabilities. Our evolutionary development caused us to overstate probabilities. We needed to inflate the risk of danger in order to stay alive. We inherited our genes from the survivors. In earlier years we were not designed to understand things. We were built to survive and procreate. And yet, now, in our more complex environment, we need to understand. Certainly in trading, we need to undertake a more accurate assessment of probabilities.

But our minds become clouded. So much combines to distort a clear assessment of the probabilities. Hope and fear alter the picture. Memories become overstated or deleted.

"There is nothing that fear or hope does not make men believe."
—Vauvenaugues

When a trader is busy hoping that she's right and fearing that she's wrong and all the while trying to support her sense of self, she has very little conscious room left to actually perceive what is happening.

As traders we're always making decisions. We make decisions as to what plan or strategy to follow, and then in the moment we again make decisions as to whether to stick with the strategy or abandon it. When we make a decision, we rarely have enough information to make that decision because the future is always unknown. That's why we're making a decision. Without sufficient knowledge, we fall back on emotions. We don't have enough facts. All decisions are in the end emotional.

If our emotional commitment to a proven methodolgy is weak, the slightest wiggle can send us rushing into a new trade or abandoning a current trade. We forget how to execute our model in the market. We forget that our job is to facilitate the decision that we've already made to follow a particular strategy.

"The size of a decision is always proportional to the inadequacy of the reason for making it."

"If information is sufficient to make the decision for us, then we, as humans, are superfluous. We are only called in to make decisions when an analysis of information is insufficient—that is to say, when we have to speculate or question or apply human values and emotions. So the human element in decisions is vital. In the end all decisions are emotional."
—Edward de Bono

If something is logically obvious, we do not have to make a decision. It's when the evidence or the supporting factors are unclear that we are forced to decide. Add to the uncertainty the demands of an unstable ego, and the decision process becomes even more difficult. An out of control ego can be devastating to any trading decision. We're already working with barely enough. Emotion and sense of self bring in many different coping mechanisms that cloud the information at hand. We distort, delete, deny, rationalize, explain away, and often imagine something that isn't there. A child could tell us the chart is hurtling downward, and yet we're busy wondering if it isn't putting in a bottom.

> *"Of all the causes which conspire to blind Man's erring judgment, and misguide the mind, What the weak head with strongest bias rules, Is pride, the never-failing vice of fools."*
> —Alexander Pope

PRIDE OBSCURES INTUITION

> *"The real purpose of scientific method is to make sure Nature hasn't misled you into thinking you know something that you actually don't."*
> —Robert Pirsig

When you're busy protecting your ego from feelings of insufficiency or when you blindly over assess your abilities, you will not be open to receiving your intuitive awareness of market action.

A knowledgeable person who lives with the market day after day can often sense on a subliminal level what the market is about to do. Some call this market savvy. Others call it intuition. I know that when I dream about a stock or a market's direction, it's almost always predictive. The problem is that I don't dream enough about the market to make it a reliable method of trading.

LOSS AVERSION

There are certain human anomalies that traders possess that effect trading and muddy clear intuition. When you add the distortions created by ego, it becomes even more difficult to trust intuition. Loss aversion effects economic intuition.

If you had to sell stock to raise money for a car purchase, would you sell the stock in which you had a double or the stock in which you were under water? Those who have analyzed thousands of accounts at discount brokerage have discovered that most people would prefer to lock in a profit, rather than realize a loss.

Apparently we derive more pain from loss than joy from winning. That makes more traders and investors willing to take small profits and "conserve" their money when they're winning, and more daring (reckless?) when they are facing a loss which they hope to avoid. Traders will seek to secure a sure gain even if it's still increasing and avoid realizing an open loss even if it's getting larger. Gamblers show the same human propensity when hoping at the end of the day to wipe out losses, they bet on longer odds, and in so doing increase the chances of making their losses bigger.

THE ENDOWMENT EFFECT

Another anomaly is that people demand more money to give up something they already have than to buy it in the first place. Such behavior has been dubbed the endowment effect. It seems that ownership creates inertia as well as overvaluation. That's why many merchants give purchasers a free trial period. They're betting that once the people have the product they will be disinclined to return it. Once owning a stock, an investor or trader has a tendency to over endow it with potential value. There is a natural reluctance to sell it. They hold the underlying thought: it's mine; it must be good.

The endowment effect is a corollary of loss aversion. We hate to lose what we already have or had. Together loss aversion and the endowment effect feed a hesitation to abandon failing projects. People feel there is too much invested to quit. The Vietnam war is an example of refusing to cut a failing enterprise in a timely manner. There was a feeling that we'd lost too much to quit. We added to a bad investment. When a trader adds to a losing position, he does the same thing.

OVERCONFIDENCE

Overconfidence distorts our perceptions. We look back and we say we knew it all along. We look forward and we think we know what will happen this time. Overconfidence causes us to miss the clues that we are indeed wrong in our prediction.

Analysts also seem to be overconfident in their views. They made some 8,000 recommendations at the end of 2000 on equities in the S & P 500. There were only 29 who recommended selling.

UNDER CONFIDENCE

Under confidence also warps clear perception. We do not trust our observations or interpretations. The under confidence can allow our minds to become prey to somebody else's prognostications. And we do not trust that we do indeed know what we know.

AN OPEN MIND

We need to approach the market with an open mind. We need to trust our methods. We need to accept that the market is indeed doing just exactly what it is doing. We need to think in terms of probabilities because that is all we have, and probabilities are enough.

Trading is not about us. It is not about keeping our ego intact. Trading is about assessing the probabilities and acting upon them in a timely way.

APPRAISING YOUR TRADING RELATIONSHIP TO PRIDE

1. Does your self-esteem rise and fall with your latest trading?

2. Have you ever taken a trade just to prove your ability as a trader?

3. Do you brag about your winning trades to others?

4. Do you try to hide your losing trades from others?

5. Do you ever make up false stories about your trading to impress others?

6. Do you worry about what other people think of you as a trader?

7. Make an honest self-assessment of your trading.

8. Compliment yourself and give yourself credit when you do something right.

9. When you make a mistake or do something that doesn't serve your trading, plan how you will correct this tomorrow or in the future. Say to yourself, "That's not like me. I can do better."

10. Notice your improvement and commit to doing better each day, week, month, and year.

SUPPORTIVE BELIEFS

- I am much more than my trading.

- I accept myself just as I am.

- I am okay just as I am no matter what anybody else thinks or says about me.

- I can learn from my trading mistakes.

- I am becoming a better trader through learning and practice.

- I am a worthy person aside from my trading and accomplishments.

- I deserve to win.

96

- I am humble in front of market forces.

- The market is bigger than I am.

- The market will always do what it wants to do, and I can make it my guide and follow along.

- No one trade will ever make me feel bad.

- No one trade will ever stop me from being and becoming who I want to be.

Chapter 6

OVERCOMING THE SIN OF ANGER

*"Anger is the most destructive of emotional responses,
for it clouds your vision the most."*
—Robert Greene

"Anger is a short madness."
—Horace

Trading in a blind rage is a good way to lose money and wear yourself out in the process. The market doesn't care about your feelings or your positions anymore than the rain cares that you've planned a picnic or the wind cares that you've just had your hair done.

One of my clients who trades in a day trading shop told me the following story.

"This one guy was losing money, and he got so mad he put his fist through the computer screen. The glass shattered all over his desk and the floor. He cut his hand, and the blood was dripping all over the glass. And we all just stared at our computer screens pretending nothing had happened. He didn't come back in for the rest of the week."

One man told me that he had to continually replace his computer mouse because he kept throwing it against the wall as he was trading.

Another trader told me how after a bad day's trading, he'd kicked over a trash can on the street. Unfortunately a policeman witnessed it. "I'm sorry sir, I'll pick it up. I had a bad day." After he cleaned it up, the cop told him to walk around the block a few times before going into the subway. "It's hot down there," he said.

Stuart Walton relates his early experience on a trading desk in Jack Schwager's *Stock Market Wizards[1]* .

"There were traders on the desk who would just scream at me all the time. Most times I didn't even know why. Maybe it was because they needed somebody to take it out on when their positions went bad, or maybe it was because I didn't do things quickly enough for them. I would go home every night upset because someone had shouted at me."

I have never heard a trader tell me that anger enhances his trading, and yet anger seems to be ubiquitous to the trading experience. Sometimes the anger is directed at the market in general or at "the idiots on the other side of the trade". Sometimes the anger is justly directed at a broker because of a truly horrendous fill.

I remember once screaming at a broker on the floor of the S&P pit. They'd filled my hundred contracts at a price that hadn't even printed. And yet all my anger did not correct the fill. They just inserted the price a half hour later. Once I heard a colleague of mine screaming at the floor in a very loud and colorful manner. I went and stood at the door of his office and listened.

He said, "Ruth, I'm sorry."

I responded, "Oh no. It's fine with me. I just want to see if it does any good."

It didn't. And it rarely does. The problem is that even justified anger clouds the mind and takes the attention away from where it needs to be— price movement and timely action.

*"He that is slow to anger is better than the mighty;
and he that ruleth his spirit than he that taketh a city."*
—Proverbs 16:32

*"Be not hasty in the spirit to be angry: for anger
resteth in the bosom of fools."*
—Ecclesiastes 7:9

We need to be slow to anger, but that does not mean we should never get angry. Anger has its just purposes.

THE USEFUL PURPOSE OF ANGER

All emotions, both positive and negative, have a valid function and purpose. Nevertheless, emotions misunderstood and misused can become exaggerated and distorted and cause enormous destruction. Anger, more than most other emotions, seems to have the power to damage both self and others. Anger, used destructively, could land a person in jail. It could cause you to hurt a person you love. Anger, expressed and unexpressed, can create enormous health problems. Before we explore the negative effects of anger, let's look at the positive function of anger.

The functional attribute of anger is that it tells you that something or somebody—possibly even yourself—has violated your standards. Anger alerts you that you are in a situation where you need to do something to protect yourself now or in the future. A prompt and reasoned action is called for.

Your fills keep coming back with enormous slippage? You need to trade another market or find another broker or another means of entering the orders.

The system you bought is losing money? You need immediately to stop trading it and verify that it does work.

The firm you trade with keeps losing your trades—particularly the ones in your favor? You need to keep close watch, check out, and if necessary change firms.

You keep violating your trading rules? You need to commit to the rules and believe in them. Then, if you still can't discipline yourself, you need to seek assistance.

The market keeps gapping against you overnight? Maybe you need to day trade, or just take a much longer view to investing and trading.

You keep losing money? You need to develop or discover better methods.

Your methods work, but you're still losing money? You need to discover where the problem lies and correct it. Perhaps you're inconsistently applying the methods.

You keep getting stuck in big losing trades? You need to find out what keeps you from recognizing the first signs that a trade has gone sour and realize that being wrong is not taking that first loss.

You get angry with the market for making you wrong? You need to realize that there is no right or wrong in trading: there are only probabilities that do or don't work out.

Somebody gave you some bad advice? Don't take that person's advice again. You don't want to be like the two fellows who received a losing tip from a broker. One guy said, "I'm going to give him a piece of my mind!" The other said, "Don't do that! He might not give us another tip!"

EFFECTIVE AND REASONABLE ACTION

Since the message of anger is that you need to take steps to protect yourself, you need to take action. But the action needs to be reasonable and effective. Too often an angry person just lashes out in the most counter-productive ways.

"Anyone can become angry—that is easy, but to be angry with the right person to the right degree at the right time for the right purpose in the right way—that is not easy."
—Aristotle

One of my weight loss clients got so angry with the weight his scale registered, he threw the scale out the window. In New York City that's a very dangerous thing to do. He could have killed somebody. In any event, it didn't get him even an ounce closer to weight reduction. The same was true of the trader who punched his fist through the monitor screen. The action only hurt himself and the computer: it didn't alleviate the loss or make him any money.

A trader can become enraged with Alan Greenspan for lowering the discount rate in the middle of the trading day when he had on a large short position. He can become livid and rail at Greenspan for disrupting the orderly markets. But what he really needs to do is get himself out of his short position as best and as quickly as he can. Then he can step back and reassess, and take the action that is most probably likely to produce a profit. The trouble is that it's hard to take meaningful action while ranting and raving.

BECOMING AWARE OF YOUR ANGER

Emotions are early warning systems. They let us know what is right and wrong in our lives. They are very precise indicators of what we want and don't want in our lives.

People have different reactions to anger as to all emotions. Some people are very at ease expressing their anger. Others feel a great need to control their anger. Still others completely repress all anger believing that it is unwarranted or wrong to even feel anger.

The first step is to be aware of your feelings. You're feeling bad? Ask yourself, "What exactly am I feeling?" If the answer is anger, observe it. Ask yourself, "What precisely am I angry about?"

You can then receive the message of anger—somebody has violated your values and you need to take effective action to protect yourself. Acknowledge the feeling and appreciate its positive purpose. It is important to be aware that you're feeling angry and to accept that feeling. There are several ways to handle any emotion. Let's look at some ways to handle anger.

First, you can deny your anger and suppress or repress it. If you do this, however, you can create depression and a range of physical ailments. In repressing your anger, you will likely suppress your joy as well. Furthermore, you won't be alert to the valid message that anger is sending you.

Second, you can dramatize your anger. You can scream, stamp, punch, quit, and so forth. In this case you're letting the emotion dictate your behavior. You're at the effect of your emotion. This is hardly the place from which you could do your best trading or thinking.

Third, you can observe and acknowledge your anger. You can learn from it. You can make a plan. What actions are most likely to resolve the difficulty?

ANGER TO CURIOSITY

After acknowledging the anger, the next step is to become curious. What can you do now or in the future to prevent this from happening again? Did you or anyone else you know ever confront and handle a similar situation effectively? In your imagination go out into the future and try several approaches. What is most likely to work for you?

TAKE ACTION

"Negative emotions like these" (anger, fear, grief) *"arise to catch our attention, to give us a Wake-Up call, and to empower us with neurological energy to do something. To take effective action."*
—L. Michael Hall, Ph.D.

It's not enough to simply run it through your mind. You need to take timely action. Change what you're doing. It may or may not work, but at least you'll get feedback and can try something else. Positive anger will produce effective action. Negative anger will produce destructive action.

Maybe the only action you need is to express yourself. Tell the offending person that their behavior or the situation is unacceptable to you. Remain as calm as you can as you draw your boundaries and explore a possible solution.

If there can be no solution, maybe the action you need to take is to remove yourself from the situation.

LOOKING AT THE BIGGER PICTURE

Nine times out of ten, if you take the long view, the anger will dissipate. Ask yourself, how important will this be tomorrow, or a week or month or year from now.

Let me tell you about a Sufi legend. As the story goes, a Sufi village was captured by a group of warriors. The captain of the warriors gathered the Sufi elders and told them that unless they could show him what would make him happy when he was sad, and sad when he was happy, the entire village would be put to death the following morning.

The Sufis built a large bonfire and all night long pondered the question: what would make people happy when they were sad and sad when they were happy? When morning came, the captain entered the village.

"Do you have the answer to my question?" he asked.

A wise man reached into his leather pouch and pulled out a gold ring and handed it to the captain.

"Why on earth do you give me gold? I have plenty of gold. I need something that will make me happy when I am sad, and sad when I am happy."

And then he looked. Inside the ring were inscribed the words *"This too shall pass."*

So it is with trading and living. When you are most euphoric, know that this will pass. When you are most desolate, know also that this will pass. Conditions are temporary. It's the long trail of trading that matters.

EMOTIONS: THE BODY'S RESPONSE TO THOUGHTS

Emotions are the somatic (bodily) response to perceptions and thoughts that we have. The emotions register in our bodies the way we are perceiving our relationship to the external world. The mental becomes physical.

We compare our internal maps of how the world or the trading should be to our experience of the world or trading. When we get less from the market experience than we expected or wanted, we will experience a negative emotion such as anger, fear, regret, remorse, or discouragement. When we receive more from the market interaction than we anticipated, then we feel positive emotions such as euphoria, confidence, satisfaction, glee, or giddiness.

Because emotions are housed in our body, they seem more real or valid than simple thoughts. And yet each emotion is simply a response to a thought. Emotions are no more or less true than the thoughts that spawn them, even when they appear to have a true reality of their own.

THE PHYSIOLOGICAL CONSEQUENCES OF ANGER

Anger signals you. It cues your body that something out there is not measuring up to the way you think it should be. It speeds up your heart rate, raises your blood pressure, and produces a flow of adrenaline. All this, of course, enables you to take quick action, and hopefully right action. It particularly helps if the action you need to take is physical, such as attacking or running away. If, however, all you need to do is pick up the phone or click a mouse, you may well have more adrenaline than you need.

If you're constantly in a physical state of high alert when your only physical outlet is to pick up a phone or click a mouse or do nothing, you will be stressing your system unnecessarily. If there is any weakness in your system, that is where the strain will occur.

Anger expressed and unexpressed can produce high blood pressure, heart strain, headaches, stomach ulcers, and skin rashes. Researchers have reported that those individuals who are habitually angry have a much higher incidence of heart attacks. In fact, research has shown that the people who are easily and repetitively angry live shorter lives.

Repressed anger can produce depression. It is anger turned on oneself. In addition, the suppression of anger is suspected of being the cause of certain auto immune diseases and various back and skeletal ailments.

Physiological manifestations of anger would be frowning, clenching the teeth, gripping the hands and raising the voice or speaking in clipped short sentences.

LOSING CONTROL IN AN ATTEMPT TO GAIN CONTROL

The angry person is seeking to establish control in a situation that is frustratingly out of control. The irony is that the angry person often not only loses further control of the situation but loses control of the self as well. The anger breeds a further loss of power to direct events.

Of course, we all know that we do not have control of the market, and it's foolish or illegal to try to control it. We do have control of what we do in the market, and how we read and react to the market. We are in danger of losing that control when anger is controlling us.

Negative anger is often caused by feelings of frustration and inferiority. The trader who gets caught up in rage or fury will only worsen his situation and lessen his self-esteem.

AN ANGRY TRADER

Janice stood there at the door to his office tossing her pale blond hair. "Come on, baby! How often do I ask you to do something for us? All I want is for you to pick up Timmy at 3:00 and bring him home. I'll be back at 5:00. It's just two hours."

"Damn it! Just two hours! Including the final hour of trading! I've told you I can't miss that. That's when I make a lot of our money."

"You said it was the beginning hour of trading. I never ask you to do anything then. Come on, baby, do it just this once."

He gave in to her. He always did. And he always regretted it. She had some kind of spell over him. Why didn't anybody ever understand how critical the trading game is?

If he worked for a corporation or a bank or something, she'd never ask him to do anything "just this once". And yet it would be easier to leave some kind of corporate political game with a slick and cagey explanation than to leave the market swirling and lurching only to come home and find himself swinging in the wind. If he took himself out, he'd miss the trade of the day. If he didn't, he'd be bull dozed. Trading is a demanding and unforgiving profession, and there are no short cuts. No exceptions. No easy ways around.

He slammed the headpiece to his phone on the desk. He'd just put on a trade and it was already going against him.

"Damn. Damn. Damn. I thought for sure this one would roll."

He felt a cold sweat on the back of his neck, a sour taste in his mouth. He'd better get out. He sure as heck didn't want to ride another one to destruction.

As soon as he got out, the trade turned around. He kicked the desk..

"Just figures. What a lousy day. If Janice hadn't started me off on the wrong foot, things would be going better. Why won't anybody give me a break?"

He knew he had to cool things down, find another trade, and get on with his day. He had to pull things together. He couldn't let anybody kill the goose that lays the golden eggs.

"There. Right there. Look how that baby's setting up. If it takes out the top of the last bar, I'll buy it."

He bought it, and just as he'd thought, it started sliding gracefully upwards. As it took out a pivot, he doubled the position.

"Come on, sweetheart, keep on keeping on. That's it, baby. Here we go!"

"What the heck! What's going on? That bastard Greenspan must be talking again. Check for news. No! It can't be!"

The trade was cratering. Just when he had nursed it so carefully. He jumped out, incising a minor profit just before it turned into a loss.

"These bastards! Why don't they leave things alone?"

And once again, he began kicking the desk. "Idiots!"

The day went on, some good, some bad. He was beginning to feel a little threadbare around the edges. Finally, around 2:30 he had on a short position that was really going his way. He didn't want to take it off, but he had to pick Timmy up at 3:00. If he put in a stop, they'd just take it out. If he left the trade in, the market would reverse at 3:00. He did the only thing he could do. He took his profits—early.

When he got home with Timmy, he saw that the market—and what should have been his short position—had really tanked. He groaned.

"What's the matter, Daddy?"

"Your mother just cost me a ton of money—again!"

When Janice got home, Timmy asked her, "Why do you always make Daddy so mad by costing him so much money?"

Before they realized it, the two of them were locked into another one of their pointless and circular fights. And this time it was in front of Timmy.

* * *

It's not at all unusual for a trader to shift his frustrations unto the people around him. Often it's the very ones he most loves, the very ones he's working for, who end up getting the blame for the day's mishaps. Nobody likes to be blamed for another person's difficulties. Very often they will dish it right back. Then the angry trader can have additional things to be upset about; and, if he's not careful, he'll take it into the next day's trading, only to have it snowball.

BLAME TO RESPONSIBILITY

"WILL ANGRY INVESTORS BLAME BUSH?" This was on the cover of U.S. News and World Report, July 22, 2002 issue. Inside the magazine were the following words:

"With millions of Americans losing money on Wall Street, including elderly and middle-aged wage earners whose pensions and 401k funds are invested in stocks and mutual funds, many people may soon be looking for someone to blame. And the targets for public wrath are easy to demonize: corporate fat cats who used accounting deceptions, insider information, and other chicanery to make big bucks while investors lost their shirts and workers lost their jobs."

Angry investors will, of course, blame Bush, blame Greenspan, blame the corporate fat cats. They will blame anybody but themselves for how they handled their funds. This will give them righteous indignation, a sense of blame-lessness, and a perceived victimhood. But it will not correct the problem.

In an attempt to get the feeling of inadequacy out of the self, the angry trader places it on situations or persons outside of herself. It's the times. It's the government. It's the market. It's the broker. It's the system. It's the guru. And so forth.

THE MONEY MANAGER AND THE ANALYST

"Damn it, man, I thought you said the earnings were going up, that the company was turning around. Now look, this is the third quarter of lower sales and pathetic earnings."

"They led me to believe earnings would be higher. I gave you the best interpretation I could on the facts as I knew them."

"The facts as you knew them were pure fictions. Why don't you just start your reports with 'Once upon a time, there was a sweet little company.' Then I'll be able to interpret it to mean a lying, thieving, decrepit organization."

"Listen, I don't have the inside scoop."

"Then why do you call yourself an analyst and spin out reams of numbers and reasonable sounding interpretations?"

"I'm an analyst, not a fortune teller."

"You're a fortune destroyer, a drivel analyzer, who just cost me a bundle."

And so it goes. The money manager blames the analyst. The analyst blames the company. Neither takes responsibility for their part in the mishap. Temporarily, it may make them feel better, but they won't improve until they each take responsibility for doing things differently in the future.

It's nothing new. Adam blamed Eve, and Eve blamed the serpent. We've been doing this for a long time.

The problem with blaming others is that you put the locus of control outside yourself. If it's that or them, you are not only not to blame, you have no control. How can you make things better if you have nothing to do with it but to rage at the unfairness of it all?

A trader needs to take full responsibility, not just with words but with thoughts and with actions. I always love it when politicians stand up claiming to take full responsibility, and then they don't. They don't do anything to correct what they've taken "full responsibility" for. In taking true full responsibility for your past or current trading, you are able to find ways to heal the future. And you are able to make changes.

Some traders blame themselves. They berate themselves. They verbally pummel themselves into the ground. But this isn't taking full responsibility to correct the situation any more than blaming others. In taking responsibility, you carefully assess the situation, and explore how you can correct it in the future. The questions to ask are: "How can I make this better in the future?" "What can I do to prevent this from happening again?"

IT'S NOT PERSONAL

"Anger only cuts off our options and the powerful cannot thrive without options. Once you train yourself not to take matters personally, and to control your emotional responses, you will have placed yourself in a position of tremendous power."
—Robert Greene

In most cases, what happens in the market has nothing to do with you personally. What you do about it, of course, does.

The probabilities suggested the market would go one way, and you positioned yourself accordingly. Something happens or doesn't happen. But the market goes the other way. Don't get mad. It's not about you.

By not taking it personally, you are able to remove yourself from the rush of indignation. And take action. Maybe even reverse your position.

FIGHTING WITH THE MARKET

Andrew's face was flushed. He started perspiring.

"@ # $ % ^ &! @ # & *! Why does this always happen to me?" he groaned.

He remembered the last time the market gapped down against him. He'd sold his position quickly only to see the market fill the gap and go on to new highs while he sat there furious that he hadn't waited.

"Oh no you don't! You're not going to get me again!"

He sat there waiting for some sign of recovery, but the market just kept sinking. His stomach and throat tightened. His stock had been three points down on the open, and he was out $3,000. Now it was five points against him, and he was losing $5,000.

"If I get out now, they'll just take it up again. I don't want to take a $5,000 hit."

He began to feel some release as the stock recovered a half point. It seemed to be basing. At least trading sideways.

"You son of a bitch, you're not going to fake me out!" he cried as the stock dropped another full point from support and paused again.

Andrew pulled off his sweater. "Man, it's hot in here!"

The S & P futures were dropping, but his stock was holding steady. He bought another 1,000 shares doubling the position.

"Now all I need is 3 points and I'm out at even. Son of a bitch!" The stock was collapsing.

He started pounding his fist on the desk. "What's the matter with these idiots? Can't they see it's over done?"

Now he was out nearly $9,000. He began to feel sick to his stomach.

"If I lose $10,000, I'll get out," he promised himself. "That's it $10,000, and I'm out of here."

Andrew sat there frozen, unable or unwilling to take his loss. He didn't even know which it was—unable or unwilling.

"Those # @ & * # program traders selling the hell out of the market and taking everything with it! Those arrogant bastards selling short on down ticks just because they're protected as program traders. Widows and orphans have to wait for an uptick to go short, but these privileged maniacs get to sell the hell out of the market whenever their computers show them an advantage."

Now the stock was ten points against him. Ten points! $14,000! Andrew pounded his other fist on the desk. The first hand hurt too much to slam it anymore.

"What a stupid way to make a living! Fighting these bastards who don't even know what they're doing."

By the end of the day Andrew knew he had to take the position off. He just couldn't go through the night wondering how it would open. And so he took his loss, all $15,400 of it.

He left the office, and almost as soon as he started down the street a homeless guy came up to him asking for money. Before he realized it, he hauled off and punched the guy.

"Get your own money! Do something. Work for a living!"

As he rounded the corner, Andrew realized he was out of control. The guy could have fought him back.

"What a life! What a day! What an idiotic way to make a living!"

* * *

You can't fight the market. You'll only lose in the long run. Andrew was no exception. He started out fighting the battle of a former trade where he'd gotten faked out, and didn't reenter. Then he was fighting this trade, but to no avail. Working harder, putting in more effort, throwing more money at it will rarely help; and in the long run will only take you down or out.

Had Andrew been able to stay present and make the market his friend, he could have captured his loss early and gone on to find another more promising opportunity. Instead he chose to fight against the tide. He lost.

FORGIVENESS AS ANTIDOTE TO ANGER

"The greatest act of healing is the act of forgiveness.
It is also the most difficult. An immutable law states,
'As you forgive, so shall you be forgiven.'
Thus, forgiveness is an act of self-kindness. It may
also heal the other person, but ultimately forgiveness
is done for yourself."
—Douglas Block

As we trade, we need to forgive ourselves our blunders, our excesses, our misdeeds. By not forgiving ourselves, we don't assure that we will never do *that* again. Rather, by clutching onto the error, we almost guarantee that we will unwittingly repeat the unfortunate behavior.

Similarly, by remaining angry with a person who has caused us trading harm, we don't liberate ourselves from that past. We do not protect ourselves by remaining angry. Instead we stay hooked to it on a psychic level in such a way that somehow we will find ourselves revisiting that or a similar situation.

Forgive, take note, take action, and go on.

ANGER INTO LEARNING

In order to alleviate destructive anger, you need to believe that you can learn as you trade, and that you can turn your insights into new behaviors that will make your trading better.

When you view your trading as a never ending process of improvement, there is no reason or need to become angry. Instead each set back is an opportunity to enhance your skills and improve the process so that you can and will become better.

SOME STEPS TO CALM ANGER

(Sometimes anger occurs with lightning rapidity. In these cases there is no time to take preventive action. Other times anger builds like a slow boil, moving from irritation or frustration into extreme displeasure or rage. It is in these times that the following procedures will lessen the expression of anger. You can also use these protocols after an angry episode to make peace with yourself.)

1. Anger has a fast tempo. Slow down your tempo by taking slow, deep breaths. Slow down your speed of self-talk and actual talk.

2. Anger is an intense emotion. Lessen the intensity by changing the words you use. For example, allow yourself to be "annoyed" rather than "infuriated". Change your tone of voice internally and externally to something softer and less strident. You can diminish the intensity by moving the pictures in your mind further away and making them duller and smaller.

3. Anger is a present and past tense emotion. Look out into the future. How important will this be next week or the week thereafter? Will it matter at all a year from now?

117

4. Anger is an away emotion: you want to avoid something. Try thinking of what you do want, what you want to go towards. And figure out a way to get what you do want.

5. Anger is a very associated emotion: you are associated to the immediate situation and to yourself and/or the other person involved in the situation. Try stepping outside of yourself and outside of the situation. Look at the situation from the eyes of a neutral observer or another wise person that you know.

6. Anger looks at the other person and what they did that was "wrong". Try looking at yourself to see how you participated in the happen stance, and see if you can change what you do, now or in the future.

EVALUATING YOUR TENDENCY TO ANGER

1. Remember a time when you got angry trading.

2. Were you angry with yourself or with others?

3. Think about other times when you got angry.

4. What did the anger cause you to do?

5. Was it helpful or destructive anger?

6. What would you rather do?

7. What would you need to believe to do this?

SUPPORTIVE BELIEFS

- I can act calmly, and still protect myself.

- I learn from my mistakes, and I forgive myself.

- I communicate my needs to others in a pleasant, effective way that makes others want to respond to my needs.

- I accept myself thoroughly and completely even when I do things that don't support my trading.

- I take honest responsibility for my own actions and correct them.

- I can be in control without getting angry.

- I am learning to master my emotions by taking the most effective action available to me.

- Tomorrow will be a better day.

---

[1] *"Stock Market Wizards,"* Jack D. Schwager; Harper Business, ISBN 0-06-662058-9.

Chapter 7

OVERCOMING THE SIN OF IMPATIENCE

"Everything comes if a man will only wait."
—Benjamin Disraeli

Impatience trips up many traders. They jump in and out of trades too quickly, too often, and too soon. This throws off the results of their trading model, and muddies the probabilities.

Some analysts believe that trading is as much about time as it is about price. If price explodes too quickly in one direction, it is likely to snap back like a rubber band pulled too far. Also, if price doesn't remain above or below a range (for example, an opening range or a reference bar) for a certain amount of time, the move becomes less significant. Some traders have a 3 or 4 period rule: if the price move they expected doesn't occur within 3 or 4 bars of their entry, they take the trade off because the probabilities have diminished. To allow time to pass takes patience.

It also takes patience to allow price to hit a predetermined entry or exit level. Again, it takes patience to wait for all the entry or exit criteria to develop.

MISS IMPATIENCE

"I ought to change my name to Impatience," Patty said as she tossed her long brown hair. "I can't stand to wait in lines to pay for anything, and I always rush across the street before the light turns green."

"As for trading, forget it. I often jump in early before my signal for entry occurs because I think I can save some money. And then the signal doesn't develop and I'm stuck trying to figure out what to do with my position."

"And I frequently grab my profit early even though every day I say I'll wait until I get a full 5 points or a signal to exit. Each day it costs me money. Each day I say I won't do it anymore. But I do."

"It's as if I'm running on high speed and the market's moving on medium speed. I try everything. I walk away from my computer screen, but then I can't stay away. I sit on my hands, but as soon as I see that wiggle against me, I pop out. I try playing slow, Baroque music, but my tempo is triple the time."

"The only time my impatience works for me is getting rid of a loser. I never sit with a losing trade. I have no tolerance for extended loss. But then often I should have just trailed my stop because the trade turns around, and I jump back in only to find myself at the end of the move."

"I make money alright, but I'd be twice as profitable if I'd just do what I say I'm going to do. I've been told that the money's made in the sitting, and I can see that it is. Maybe I should take a course in how to sit. Can you teach a Mexican jumping bean to sit still?"

"How poor are they that have not patience!
What wound did ever heal but by degrees?"
—William Shakespeare

It's understandable that a trader will try to get ahead of the game by moving ahead of her exact entry or exit signals. She can be so sure that the market is going to do something, that she attempts to get a head start, a presumed better price. The truth is she really doesn't know what the market will do. And the probabilities are not in alignment until her preset criteria occur.

JUMPING ON THE TIGER'S BACK

"Look," says John, "I used to be frozen. I just couldn't pull the trigger on a trade. I'd wait and wait for confirmation until I had enough confidence to put on the trade, and even then I couldn't do it. It would seem like something terrible would happen if I lost. It wasn't the money. I'm not afraid to spend money or even lose it. It was more like if I lost, I'd prove I couldn't be a trader, and I'd have to do something else.

"Well, speak about not feeling up to the job! I began to feel like a total failure watching my system make money and me just sitting there. I told myself, 'You must take the next trade!' Naturally, I didn't, and things just got worse. I felt like an idiot."

"Finally, I couldn't stand it any longer. The fear was paralyzing me. Each time I saw the signal developing, I'd get that sick, inadequate feeling wondering whether I'd be up to pulling the trigger when the time arrived. I didn't want to feel like that, so I started jumping into the trades early. The problem was sometimes the signals didn't develop, and I had to figure out what to do with the trade I didn't want."

"Quite frankly, even if I lost, I didn't feel half as bad as missing the trade. Now I have a new problem. I jump into trades early so I don't have to wait in fear. I feel like a guy sitting in a tree with a tiger down below. Since I can't stand hiding up there in fear, I just jump on the tiger's back."

MYRIAD MOTIVATIONS

"Fools rush in where angels fear to tread."
—Alexander Pope

The impatient trader has many different motivations. Sometimes it's the fear of missing a trade or not acting in a timely fashion. Sometimes it's simply the fear of missing out.

A trader can have a sense of urgency. This urgency can be built upon scarcity, a feeling that there won't be enough opportunities. It can also be built upon greed—that there's money to be made, and it has to be made *now.*

Some traders are in a hurry. They want to make the money, and they want to make it today. Trading has the false appeal of a get-rich-quick-scheme. If you're in a hurry to make money trading, you'll over trade in terms of size and frequency. Instead of creating rapid wealth, you'll create a rapid deficit. You need to work on the notion of getting rich slowly and consistently.

Sometimes a trader's urgency comes from a mistaken work ethic. There's money to be made, and we'd better get to work. The old notion of long and hard work doesn't apply in trading. After all, we're not digging ditches or washing floors. We're waiting for an opportunity to present itself, and then, and only then, do we act. We've gotten our job description wrong. We don't need to get in there and produce trades. We need to wait until we see a high probability trade.

LEARNING TO WAIT

"They also sere who only stand and wait."
—John Milton

It can get boring sitting there and waiting. Some traders just love the action for the action's sake. Others need to trade in order to feel alive. They love the excitement. Unfortunately, sometimes they get more excitement than they bargained for.

Timing is a central a part of trading, and it takes patience to secure the accurate timing of your methods. Sometimes you have to wait and wait for a valid entry signal to mature. Some traders cast around for something to do while they wait for the important signal. They make up trades and jump in here or there just to see what happens. This severely dilutes the profitability of their trading. I also know traders who make the bulk of their money in the opening and closing hour of trading and spend the rest of the day giving it back.

It takes patience to sit with a trade until your methods tell you it's time to take it off. Those who can sit through the wiggles and the bumps can be richly rewarded. One really good trade can make the trading day, week, or year. There's the 80-20 rule that tells us 80% of the profits are made on 20% of the trades. Since we don't know which are the 20% that will make us the big money, we need to stay with them all. Too often traders cash out early just for the comfort of having a profit or because they fear giving up what they already have.

What do we know about trading? We know that those who take many small losses and have a few big winning trades make money over time. We also know that those who lose money trading take a lot of small profits and have a few big losers. You can go broke taking a profit, contrary to what many traders think.

What does this teach us? We need to be impatient with losing trades and patient with winning trades. We need to be serene waiting for those high probability opportunities to develop. And when we identify a strong opportunity, we need to act quickly and aggressively. We need to know when to press and when to hold back.

A LIMTED WORLD VIEW

Greed causes many traders to be impatient. Underneath the greed is a notion that there is not nor will not be enough. The thought that there is not enough to go around, creates a restless urgency. You need to get yours, and you need to get it *now*.

If you can view the world as abundant with opportunity and riches rather than scarce and severely limited, that sense of ferocious urgency will diminish. When you perceive trading as rich with unending opportunity you can wait for trades to set up and profits to develop. You are enough. You have enough. And there will be enough.

RUSHING TO DISASTER

He was dreaming, he knew. In life things just aren't this bizarre. He was stumping along the bottom with his head barely above water. His computers were floating out to sea. Somehow he just kept bumping and thrusting along the bottom in an effort to reach them before they got out too far to reach. For some unknown reason he didn't get horizontal and swim quickly to them. Maybe it was because he was busy instructing some unknown and unseen person about the appropriate way to trade his system.

His alarm went off. It was a harsh call to reality. He used to call his clock an opportunity clock and the alarm a call to action. But today he dubbed it an alarm. He wanted to finish the dream, to get the computers and finish the instruction; but he realized he had to get going. The currencies were opening, and he needed to get his orders in.

As Tom was getting dressed he told himself to take his time today and just wait and see how things develop. He didn't want to rush in like he did yesterday and find himself drowning in a quick market reversal. He remembered instructing the person in his dream to wait half the period of the opening range to make sure the breakout was for real. Maybe he could practice what he preached.

But once again he was darned if he could wait. Prices seemed to be going by too quickly. He felt he needed to get in before they got away from him. It seemed like something terrible would happen if he missed the move. This time it worked. He wasn't too early. He shorted the Japanese Yen, and had a good ride.

By the time the S & P opened, he was ready to go again. "Wait, wait, wait," he said to himself. He didn't want to get caught in a snap back the way he did yesterday and the day before. Oh, this was going to be good. He bought five e-mini's at the market and put his stop at the other end of the opening range. On any pull back, he'd add another 5. And that's what he did only to be stopped out of all ten. Now he had to get himself short and make the money back. Even as he was once again saying "wait", he was placing his orders. It happened a second time. The prices retraced immediately, and he lost again.

Tom knew that his methods called for him to let a move mature. Time and again his urgency not to miss out thrust him headlong into a churning market before direction had time to settle down. He was losing money, and still he couldn't stop himself. He knew how to trade, and at the end of every day he confidently looked forward to the next day, but when the next day came, he repeated his frantic rush to trade, and to trade badly at that.

***

Greed and a sense of insufficiency were forcing Tom's trades. As traders we want to have a sense of abundance of time, money, and opportunity. If we don't think we have enough time to make the money, we'll over trade in terms of size and frequency.

Ask yourself how you feel about time. Do you have a sense of hurriedness, or do you feel there is enough time to accomplish what you want? Remember, we all have all the time there is. Each day we have 24 full and complete hours to use and enjoy. We can't borrow from tomorrow and we don't owe any of today's time to yesterday,

SEVEN C'S FOR TIMELINESS

CLARITY

To trade effectively you need clarity of vision. You want to see both the big picture and the smaller picture at the same time. You want to identify the significant detail and dismiss insignificant details as mere distractions. You can consider both long and short arguments at the same time, and still act in accordance with your methods. With clarity, impatience subsided.

It's important to believe what you see. It doesn't matter how much you don't want to believe what you're seeing—you need to accept it. In trading honesty is your first level of protection. You might say, "I'm wrong! I'm so wrong, I'm going the other way!" On the other hand, you might say, "This is just a small move, a typical fake out. I'm not going to let it scare me out." How do you know? You perceive what the markets are showing you, and you are aware of what your methods are telling you to do.

In trading we learn from the past and bring those understandings into the present. The only time frame in which we can trade is the present, and so we need to stay, as some have said, in "the church of what is happening now." Above all, we need to be realistic in the present even as we stay optimistic about the future of our trading.

CALM

Trading is fun and exciting, but even as you enjoy the exhilaration of the trade, you can remain calm. Being calm, you can be patient. Calmness comes from trust. If you can trust your methods to give you an edge, and if you can trust yourself to implement your methods, you can remain serene. If you can't trust yourself or your methods, you would be well advised not to trade.

Calmness also comes by interpreting your trading as a process that extends over time. One trade is but one small link in a long chain. Each trade is like a single point in a game. It doesn't win or lose the game. And each game is just one in a long season.

CONSISTENCY

Impatience breeds inconsistency. Inconsistency is no better than trading from the seat of your pants. Inconsistency skews the probabilities against you.

Each morning before trading, go over you trading plan. Assess your view of the day. Set your intention to trade your plan. Accept, really accept, the inevitability that there could be losses even as you expect success.

You have decided what your strategy is, now all you have to do is facilitate that strategy. You prepare to take your orders from your strategy and the market. With consistency, the probabilities will kick in over time and lead you to your much deserved profits. Be patient.

COURAGE

It takes courage to stay with a winning trade and risk losing the bird in the hand to garner the two in the bush. It also takes a different kind of courage to sit and wait for a trade to develop while it seems the price is running away from you or you could grab it at a better price.

I'm talking about smart courage. I don't mean that kind of stubborn courage that stays with a losing position—or even worse, adds to it. There is a kind of false courage that gets stuck with some kind of preconceived idea that flies in the face of actual market action. No, courage must be courage that follows your strategy and stays within your time frame for trading.

There's another kind of courage, and that is the courage to face your own inadequacies or weaknesses in the market. Does your strategy really work? Can you consistently follow that strategy? By making excuses for yourself or rationalizing your behavior, you will not be able to correct the situation and make your trading better. Admit you've been wrong and find a way to change in the future.

CAUTION

Caution can help you balance your impatience. Think of the yellow light in the stop and go lights. It's not stop. It's not go. But it is a warning to get ready to shift. They teach drivers in driving classes to ask when they see the yellow light, "Do I have time to stop?" This is a very different kind of question than, "Can I make it?"

The conundrum of trading is that we must be bold, but not too bold. Caution is your handmaiden or your buddy with whom you trade. Caution means putting in stops, stopping at the red light. Caution means waiting for the green light before going. Caution is your antidote to reckless rushing.

COMMITMENT

Excellence requires commitment. You commit to each aspect of trading—from research to execution. You can't just go in and sling trades around. Nor can you fail to show up each day, and arrive each day on time fully prepared.

Trading is a job, a profession, or as they say about the law, a jealous mistress. It requires attention and discipline.

If you have an impatient bent, you can heal that by committing yourself to the entire process and each of the small steps that make up the totality of the trading experience. It has been said that when we commit, the universe conspires to assist us. You don't know what to do? Find out what methods work and check them out. You can't execute your methods properly? Find a coach who can help you train yourself. And stay with it until you have the consistent success you desire.

CONFIDENCE

Confidence gives you a timeless sense of time. You know what your strategies can do for you. You know that the market can do anything. Confidently you act in the now and let trades develop as they will.

The confident trader doesn't need to be restless and pushing. There's a knowledge that all things will come in time. If your strategies have worked in the past, the likely probability is that they will work in the future. A temporary losing streak doesn't mean failure.

Confidence grows through recognition. Catch yourself doing something right. Notice it. Compliment yourself. You can ask yourself certain questions at the end of a trading day that will build assurance. What did I do that was effective? In what ways did I follow my rules? What can I do differently that will make me trade better tomorrow?

Compare yourself to yourself, not to others that you know or have read about. Use helpful questions to direct your focus. In what ways am I getting better? How can I become even better?

Confidence comes with experience. You practice real time on paper. Then you practice trading small amounts of money. Gradually you increase your size. When you have made a mistake, you mentally practice doing it right. Every morning and every evening you mentally rehearse right action within your trading strategy. And don't forget to praise yourself each time you do something right.

Today is just another day in a lifetime of trading. Today you can do your best, having learned from the past. Today you can mark your time being quick and steady as circumstances require because you are confident of the bright future of your trading. You are fully trusting that you will win over time. And so, you have a sense of everything happening in it's own sweet time.

Confidence allows you to be present in the moment. It allows you to concentrate on present occurrences and trust your strategy and the philosophy behind your method. It allows you to act and do what needs to be done and not done in a timely and dauntless way.

ASSESSING YOUR LEVEL OF IMPATIENCE

1. Do you wait for your predetermined signal to exit a trade?

2. Do you enter trades early with insufficient evidence?

3. Do you change your trading plan after the market starts trading?

4. Can you wait for the market to fill you at your price?

5. Do you feel rushed or hurried as you trade?

6. Do you sometimes trade just to have something to do?

7. How does this help or hurt your trading?

8. One way to slow things down is to write each day's trading plan in advance.

9. Set your firm intention to follow your plan.

10. At the first violation of the trading plan, take a break, and recommit to a steady application of the plan.

SUPPORTIVE BELIEFS

Time is on my side.

I have all the time I need to accomplish what I want.

The world is an abundant place.

The market is a rich source of unending opportunity.

I can be in alignment with the quiet part of me even as I watch the market.

The market moves in its own rhythm, and I can move fast or slow depending on it's pace.

A person is able to create wealth slowly through trading.

Chapter 8

IDENTIFYING YOUR OWN MAJOR TRADING SINS

"*History is Philosophy teaching by examples.*"
—Thucydides

Each person has certain behaviors and modes of thinking that tend to repeat and interfere with effective trading. What behaviors effect your trading negatively?

The following are some possible actions that could interfere with your trading success. Make a check after each one that applies to you.

NEGATIVE TRADING BEHAVIORS

- Over Trading In Size

- Jumping The Gun

- Hesitating

- Skipping Trades

- Being In A Hurry

- Trading Without Proper Preparation

- Getting Stuck In A Losing Trade

- Whipsawing

- Breaking Your Trading Rules

- Shooting From The Hip

- Over Interpreting

- Discounting

- Trading A Scenario Without Reference to Price

- Trading Heedlessly

- Trading Wildly

- Abandoning Your Trading Plan

- Not Having A Trading Plan

- Switching Strategies Frequently

- Not Having A Proven Strategy

- Not Pulling The Trigger

- Not Believing The Evidence The Market Provides

- Blindly Believing A Story You Tell Yourself

- Blindly Believing A Story Somebody Else Tells You

- Becoming Impulsive

- Not Verifying A System Or Method Before You Trade It

- Over Researching

- Getting Stuck In Endless Paper Trading

- Using Trading As A Spectator Sport

- Jumping In Before You Research

- Jumping In Before You Think

- Trading Too Small

- Trading Too Big

- Grabbing Profits Too Soon

- Getting Careless

- Being Too Careful

- Not Adding To A Winning Trade

- Trading Heavier When Losing

- Forcing Trades

- Getting Trigger Happy

- Gulping Profits Too Soon

- Adding To A Losing Trade

- Overtrading In Terms of Frequency

- Sticking With A Losing System

- Sticking With A Broker That Gives You Bad Fills

- Expecting Or Letting Your Broker Tell You What To Do

- Not Making Trading A Priority

- Worrying What Others Will Think

- Trading With Borrowed Money

- Trading With Insufficient Risk Capital

- Trading With Money You Need To Live On

- Holding Unrealistic Expectations

- Engaging In Negative and Destructive Self Talk

- Becoming Despondent About Your Trading Results

- Wanting Certainty Before You Trade

- Disregarding Probabilities

- Fooling Yourself About Your Trading

- Not Keeping Proper Records

- Not Acknowledging Mistakes

- Not Learning From Mistakes

- Repeating Mistakes

- Engaging In Self Pity

- Blaming Others

- Getting Envious Of Other Traders

- Giving Up Periodically

- Giving Up Period

- Resisting Loss

- Feeling Shame For Loss

- Lying And Covering Up Results

- Becoming Pessimistic About The Future Of Your Trading

- Being Unrealistic About Your Present Trading

- Tying Self Worth To Trading

- Bragging About Trading

- Being Unduly Secretive About Trading

- Using Trading To Inflate Your Ego

- Letting Trading Interfere With A Full And Balanced Life

- Letting Life Interfere With Full And Balanced Trading

- Using Trading To Avoid Living

- Doing Anything Unethical Regarding Your Trading

- Doing What Doesn't Work

- Not Continuing To Do What Does Work

- Getting Reckless

- Getting Overcautious

- Letting Others Put You Down Re Your Trading

- Putting Yourself Down Re Your Trading

- Waiting to Respect Yourself Until You Succeed With Trading

- Being Unorganized In Your Efforts

- Trading For The Sake Of Trading

- Letting Distractions Take Your Attention Away From Trading

- Not Specializing

- Not Executing With Precision

- Forgetting To Cancel Stops After A Trade Is Off

- Not Using Stops To Protect Against Undue Loss

- Being Careless With Orders: Not Treating Them As Live Ammunition

- Behaving In Inconsistent Ways

- Fighting Yourself

- Fighting The Market

- Fighting Your Methods

- Making Careless Errors

- Personifying the Market

- Projecting Your own feelings on the market

- Other

Go over each of the behaviors you have checked, and scale them from 1 - 10 as to severity. Let 10 represent the most harmful to your trading.

YOUR PERSONAL SEVEN DEADLY BEHAVIORS

Let the top seven represent your personal Seven Deadly Behaviors. Write them in the spaces provided below.

1. _____

2. _____

3. _____

4. _____

5. _____

6. _____

7. _____

DESTRUCTIVE ATTITUDES AND EMOTIONS UNDERLIE UNWANTED BEHAVIORS

Beneath each of these behaviors is an attitude or emotion, that motivates the action. Ask yourself what underlies your negative trading behaviors? In other words, what is the emotional or mental tendency that causes you to perform the actions that interfere with your trading success?

You might have included some of the original deadly sins. You might have listed completely different transgressions. The following are certain attitudes and emotions that could underlie your unhelpful behaviors

POSSIBLE HARMFUL DISPOSITIONS OF MIND AND FEELING

- Greed
- Fear
- Anger
- Pride
- Impatience
- Recklessness
- Perfectionism
- Cowardice
- Impulsiveness
- Dogmatism
- Egotism
- Laziness
- Urgency
- Self Doubt
- Denial
- Timidity
- Feeling Unworthy
- Being Unrealistic
- Self Delusion

- Stubbornness
- Bias
- Carelessness
- Absent Mindedness
- Lack of Discipline
- Self Indulgence
- Obsession
- Grandiosity
- Wanting Instant Gratification
- Procrastination
- Suggestibility
- Personal Insecurity
- Financial Insecurity
- Taking The Short View
- Risk Aversity
- Feeling Alive Only When At Risk
- Envy
- Covetousness
- Addiction
- Self Absorption
- Narcissism
- Dishonesty
- World View of Scarcity
- Anything Else You Think or Feel

YOUR PERSONAL SEVEN DEADLY SINS

Write down the dominant disposition of mind or feeling that motivates each of your negative trading behaviors.

1. _____

2. _____

3. _____

4. _____

5. _____

6. _____

7. _____

PREFERRED TRADING BEHAVIORS

Ask yourself what action would you rather take in place of each of your Seven Deadly Trading Behaviors.

1. _____

2. _____

3. _____

4. _____

5. _____

6. _____

7. _____

SUPPORTIVE POSITIVE EMOTIONS

What would you have to feel in order to consistently perform in your preferred manner? Write down the emotions that would support each of your chosen trading behaviors.

1. _____

2. _____

3. _____

4. _____

5. _____

6. _____

7. _____

8. _____

SUPPORTIVE POSITIVE BELIEFS

Now ask yourself what would you need to believe in order to feel that way. Write down each belief.

1. _____

2. _____

3. _____

4. _____

5. _____

6. _____

7. _____

CREATING A VISION OF YOUR TRADING FUTURE

Take time to visualize each of your chosen beliefs as already being true for you. See yourself acting as you would chose to behave while trading as if these beliefs were true for you. Observe yourself feeling in the manner that would automatically spring from your new beliefs.

This new vision will provide the pulling power for your new plan of action.

Chapter 9

A BALANCING ACT

We all have many different trading sins. Sometimes they repeat and repeat and repeat and become the scourge of our trading. We wonder, will we ever overcome this damaging behavior. Other times we do something harmful that's completely uncharacteristic, and we find ourselves surprised that we did that.

It's a human condition to fall short of our desires and expectations. And so we do. What, I am asked, would the model trader be like? The model trader would have a balance of many attributes and keep those qualities in balance. He or she would be almost godlike in ability to handle and modify the emotional extremes of trading. No wonder we fall short. We will continue to be less than ideal, because we are, alas, wonderfully human. Still, we can aspire to be among the best of traders, so let us look at an ideal trader.

A MODEL TRADER

The successful trader puts first things first. Before he launches into the market he finds out how to trade. He learns from others what strategies work for them. He develops a strategy or set of strategies that suit his style, and he practices using them. A strategy does you no good if you don't use it. He combines trading with research. As he trades, he learns and adjusts his behavior and modifies his strategies. He sees his trading as a work in progress.

Beneath his strategies he has guidelines that give him a directional bias in different time frames. He stays within the time frame or frames in which he is trading. He keeps the chart sizes separate in his mind. For example, he might be day trading from a five minute chart and swing trading from a daily chart. He is able to distinguish time frames and go separate ways at the same time.

He has rock solid money management principles that guide how much of his capital is allocated to any one approach or idea. Because of this no one horrendous random event or situation can bring him down. There is a wildness lurking out there, and he never knows when it will attack his trade or system, so he protects himself with appropriate size and protective stops.

His game plan and the strategy, which he certainly has, are balanced by discretion. Nothing is rigidly cast in stone. He knows when to abandon a game plan and when to modify a strategy. However, he seldom does this. He knows that his strategies and game plan are his road map for success.

Our model trader is a risk taker, and is willing to risk in order to win. She balances risk taking with caution so she never runs over into recklessness. At the same time she balances her caution with the joy of the hunt so she never gets trapped into inaction or trading too small to make a difference.

She is courageous but not foolhardy. She employs a wise courage as she risks for an expected reward. Even when she feels tentative and fearful, she can take action. She maintains a nothing-ventured-nothing-gained attitude, which she balances with caution. She is both careful and brave. She knows better than to set out to be an super sized hero.

She is self-directed. She has a strong internal frame of reference. She is often ahead of the crowd. She is able to see things from a unique perspective. She takes responsibility for her trading. Nevertheless, she balances her self-direction by listening and by being open to what is going on. Other's opinions are in turn moderated by her own judgements.

She is able to go against the flow when her judgement tells her this is the way to go. She is capable of contrary thinking. Nevertheless, she balances this with a true belief that her friend is indeed the trend. And she can stay with a trend until her indicators tell her it's over.

148

She is a decision-maker. She is able to make decisions in a timely manner, and she understands that no decision at all amounts to a decision not to make a decision. She realizes that decisions are only made when an evaluation is necessary, when there is not enough evidence to have a foregone conclusion. If she knew that this trade would be a certain winner, she would not have to make a decision. All she has is a preponderance of the evidence. Even as she decides, she is able to take her marching orders from her system. Her rules guide her decisions.

This special trader knows his trading rules, and he follows them. His rules are his trading blueprint. He architected his rules when he crafted his system. His rules help him to make sense out of the market. They give logic to the madness. In addition, they give him consistency. Therefore he follows his rules. Still, he knows when to break and bend the rules. Therein lies the artistry.

He is an artist with his trading. Trading is an art as well as a science. And so. he is also a scientist in his trading. He is a scientific artist and an artistic scientist. He thinks with both his linear left brain and his creative right brain. He trades from the whole brain.

His intuition, based on millions of hours of watching and trading markets, gives him a knowledge that goes beyond his conscious thinking. He trusts his instincts and can often trade on savvy hunches. However, he balances his intuition with clear linear thinking based upon information available and the signals of his indicators and guidelines.

He has integrity. He does what he says he'll do, and he is what he says he is. He is honest. He has no need to cheat. He doesn't lie to himself or others. He has no need to make up excuses. He understands that excuses only keep him from improving. His integrity, however, does not keep him from going to the edge. He can be shark like when he spots a vulnerability.

Our prototype trader sees clearly. She gathers up facts and news even as she watches the market's response. She not only sees what is actually going on, she can balance that with a vision of what might possibly happen next. She can imagine the next step even as she carefully monitors current action.

She thinks in probabilities. She knows that's all she has to guide her assessments of future action are the probabilities. She balances the probabilities against past and current movement.

She not only sees clearly, she believes what she sees. If she hears herself saying, "I don't believe this," she quickly adds, "It's happening. I better believe it: it's true." Yet even as she accepts as true what she is seeing, she always expects change. There is, she knows, an inertia in prices. Something set in motion in one direction will tend to continue in that direction. Something standing still will remain in place. Until it shifts. She trusts the momentum or lack thereof even as she expects a shift in the winds of motion.

She trusts her trading methods because she has verified that they have made money in the past. She balances this trust with a healthy skepticism. After all, times change, markets change. But until they prove themselves inadequate, she trusts them. She has decided in advance what would have to happen before she would abandon them.

She not only trusts her methods, she trusts herself. She knows she will act in a timely fashion to protect herself and to capture an opportunity. She understands she needs to protect her capital so she can stay in the game, and she also realizes that the whole point of trading is to make money by entering the market. She goes towards profit even as she limits loss. She trusts herself to handle anything that comes up. Nevertheless, she understands and admits her weaknesses. She works on strengthening her weaknesses.

If she has a particular weakness such as occasional reckless trade or a rare occasion of freezing up and not being able to act, she works to improve her vulnerabilities. She uses mental rehearsal and various self-training exercises. If she cannot do it alone, she enlists the help of a psychological mentor.

If she has problems with her strategy for trading, she looks for something better that will work. Whatever kind of help she needs, whether books, courses, ready made systems, or a mentor, she seeks it out and takes advantage of what she determines to be the best.

She is always improving even as she trades with what she is and has. She knows we're never all we can be and still we're good enough just as we are. She accepts herself even as she seeks to improve. All she can do and all she can be is all she can do and all she can be. And all she can do and be is enough.

She accepts the imperfections in herself even as she strives to be perfect. She utilizes approximations of trading even as she tries to get it right.

Our exemplary trader is flexible even as he is steady. He follows his strategy uniformly and will make changes—but rarely—when he sees a way to improve them.

He knows when to press and when to stand aside. If it's a very high probability opportunity, he'll step on the gas. If he knows it's probably a dumb trade but he wants to take it anyway, he'll trade lightly and not risk much.

He is slow and steady holding unto his profits, and he's quick to take a loss. He's patient with his winners and impatient with his losers.

Our trader takes his marching orders from his system. His system is the boss, and he's the employee. He has the discipline of obedience. He balances his faithfulness to his system with an overlay of discretion. He is not rule bound, but he his rule guided. There may be times when it's best to override the system, but he keeps in mind that opinions don't have stops. If he does override his system, and it turns out to have been the wrong thing to have done, he forgives himself.

He always forgives himself even as he strives to do better. He holds himself to a high standard, and pardons himself when he doesn't live up to it. He accepts himself totally and completely even as he recognizes his flaws.

It's just a game. It's only money. But it's his game and it's his money, or it was his money. He knows it does no good to berate and belittle himself. That won't make him or the situation one whit better. He does what he can do: he commits to doing better the next time.

He learns from the past—what works and what doesn't work. And then he relearns it and relearns it yet again. He stays in the present because that is the only time frame in which you can actually trade. He remains focused in the present. This is happening now. That is not happening now. His indicators or the patterns tell him what might happen in the future, but he knows he doesn't know for sure what the next move will be.

In the present, he is realistic about his trading and the markets. He is optimistic about the future of this trade and all his trading. That's how he handles time. He learns from the past, he is honestly perceptive in the present, and he's fully optimistic about the future.

He looks at the big picture even as he looks for the significant details. He doesn't get caught up in every little wiggle because he comprehends how markets move. He knows what details are important and what are not.

He stays in his time frame even as he keeps the larger time frame in the back of his mind. He assesses the big picture and the significant detail that apply to his chosen time frame. He understands that only losers will look at the one minute chart when they placed their trade off a daily chart or look at the weekly chart when they placed their trade from a three minute chart.

He calibrates the information he receives from different sources. He is aware of the technical picture and fundamental considerations. He acts on whatever he has at any given time. He realizes that by the time he and everyone else knows why the market's moving, it's frequently too late.

He can hold in his mind viewpoints that are diametrically opposed. He can make a case for the long or the short side. But still he is able to take action based on his proven strategies.

Our model trader works with her emotions. She keeps them in check even as she feels them. Emotions are an intrinsic part of being human and they cannot be suppressed without doing damage. Still, she doesn't let them take over the trading. She holds sufficient distance from her trading results, so that she doesn't become incapacitated or get out of hand. She does not live each day on an emotional roller coaster, although she does occasionally feel the high arousal emotions of fear and excitement. They are an important part of being and staying alive as a trader. Sometimes she feels the low arousal emotions of boredom and relaxation. She keeps these under control by moving around or having something else to do as she still keeps an eye on the market.

She loves trading. She loves the challenge, and she loves the freshness of each trading day. Trading for her is pleasurable. Nevertheless, she knows that pain will come; and she has a high tolerance for pain. She also knows that both the pain and the pleasure will pass. This gives her peace and staying power.

She is a doer and a thinker. She can research and execute the research. When she trades, she puts on her trader hat. When she researches, she wears the researcher cap. She keeps the two functions separate. She doesn't trade the research before it's complete, and she doesn't stop and begin research while she's in the middle of her trading. If she spots something interesting, she'll make a note and get to it later.

She has a high degree of confidence. She is confident in her skills as well as her ability to improve those skills. She trusts the trading process. But she is not overconfident: she remains humble before the market forces.

She's humble as a trader, because she's aware that anything could happen. A random event could strike like a bolt from the blue. Even so, she believes she deserves to win, and she expects to win.

She is comfortable with uncertainty, even as she's confident in the power of her strategy to guide her. She leans on her strategy. She accepts loss as inevitable and a natural cost of trading, but she expects to win. She is comfortable both winning and losing.

Our ideal trader takes care of his physical health. He exercises, eats healthful foods in the right amount, and gets sufficient sleep. His physical being is important to him, and he keeps himself in shape. Even here, though, he practices moderation. Some days he skips the exercise. Occasionally he'll overindulge with food or drink. Some times he'll party during the week. Most of the time, however, his regime supports his healthy, health goals.

He practices good mental health. He doesn't worry about things he can do nothing about. He keeps his mind alert. He is continually learning. He asks himself supportive questions. What's causing the problem? How can I correct it? How can I become an even better trader? What is the question I should be asking right now? What is useful or good about the situation?

He is conscientious and goal oriented. He knows what he wants from his trading, and he does whatever it takes to succeed. At the same time, he realizes that he is more than his trading. He has outside interests, and enjoys his time away from the markets. He spends quality time with his family, and he nourishes his friendships.

Above all, our model trader believes in himself and herself. He and she hold supportive beliefs about themselves and the trading.

SUPPORTIVE BELIEFS

Trading is an enjoyable activity that is challenging and can be extremely rewarding.

A lot of money can be made trading winning methods.

Trading provides unlimited potential for wealth and self-development.

I have the ability to identify and trade a winning method.

I am capable of mastering the trading game.

With practice and learning, I can become the trader I choose to be.

I consistently trade my chosen methods with confidence, trust, and discipline.

I focus and trade with skill.

I plan my trade, and trade my plan, and I do it with heart and vigor.

I trade in order to create and sustain financial and personal abundance and security.

I trade to make a living and because I enjoy it.

I trade because I have important things to do with my profits.

I am (becoming) a consummate trader.

I am (becoming) a successful trader.

I am (becoming) a master of trading.

PEAK PERFORMANCE COACHING PROGRAM

IF YOU ARE NOT COMPLETELY SATISFIED WITH YOUR MINDSET FOR TRADING, GIVE ME A CALL.

WANTED: TRADERS WHO ARE READY FOR BREAKTHROUGH SUCCESS!

Do you continue to make the same and similar mistakes in your trading? Do you sometimes wonder if you are your own worst enemy in the markets? Are you fed up with blocking your own profitability? Or do you simply want insurance that you can stay at the top of your game?

Only those traders who are commited to financial and individual freedom invest in themselves by hiring me as a personal self-development trading coach. Their investment rewards them exponentially.

While my coaching progam does not teach entry and exit strategies, it does assist you in executing your own proven strategy. You learn how to do what you already know to do. In other words, you become as good as your methods. You begin to trade with trust, confidence, courage, and a reliable consistency.

Your psychological makeup is the major factor that makes or breaks you as a trader. I know this runs contrary to the popular belief that it's the technical system that holds the magic. In truth, learning to run your mind and emotions is the single most important key to your trading results. Your mindset is the multiplier of your trading profits and losses.

Call me at 1-800-692-0080 to discuss whether or not this program is right for you. The openings are limited, so call now, but only call if you are prepared to make powerful changes in your life and your trading.

Audio Course

Easy Way To Better Trading Results

You know how to think about your trading, but do you really think that way?

Internalize your knowledge by using these self-hypnosis tapes. Through repeated listening you alter your unconscious associations and begin to think like a winner. You use mental rehearsal to make automatic responses based on good trading principles. You diminish the power of old fears that have been holding you back. You become optimistic about the future of your trading.

Power Trading combines conscious and unconscious learning. You learn how to consciously think as you trade and you also learn solid trading principles that operate from the powerful unconscious mind. It is a complete system for managing your mind to make money.

There are three albums of tapes: *Inside Secrets of Winning Power Traders, Anatomy of Losing Trading,* and *Power Trading for Power Profits.* You'll also get my manual, *Complete Guide to Trader Trouble Shooting.* The first 70 who respond will also get a one hour phone consultation with me (a $300 Value) and an individualized tape addressed to their special wants and needs. The cost for the full course is $477. The value is unlimited. Call me at 1-800-692-0080 today to order.

Ruth Barrons Roosevelt, J.D.
165 William Street
NY, NY 10038
1-800-692-0080
fax: 212-732-3482
http://www.RuthRoosevelt.com

Not only does the book show you how to think and what to think. It shows you how to do it. It gives specific techniques for making the essential mind shifts that enable you to create a mental advantage. Trading is, after all, mind over markets, quick action, clear thinking, and an unclouded intent to win.

Ruth Barrons Roosevelt, a futures trader and international psychological trading coach, shows traders how to manage emotions, resolve conflicts, divorce ego, discover and change limiting beliefs, and execute a winning system with confidence.

Success leaves clues. Ruth interviews super traders Linda Bradford Rashke, Michael McCarthy, and Max Ansbacher. They talk extensively and openly about their experience and their own approach to trading.

The book is a good read, interesting from beginning to end. Here's what her colleagues say about it:

Mark Douglas: True to its title, Ruth has done an exceptional job. Her explanations are clear and concise, but most of all I think some of her techniques are brilliant. Thanks for sharing, Ruth. This book is a real credit to the industry.

Adrienne Toghraie: An exceptional psychological handbook for traders to identify and resolve some of the major issues which sabotage their discipline and therefore their success.

Van K Tharp, Ph.D.: Commitment, Beliefs, Emotions, Conflict Resolution and the Environment are just a few of the many critical topics covered in Ruth Roosevelt's interesting new book.

VIEW OF TABLE OF CONTENTS FOR EXCEPTIONAL TRADING

Chapter One
COMMITMENT TO TRADING EXCELLENCE

Trading as a business and profession that requires a serious commitment. A test to determine one's own commitment to the trading endeavor. An exploration of one's intentions with respect to successful trading. Building a commitment.

Chapter Two
WINNERS AND LOSERS: A PSYCHOLOGICAL PORTRAIT

A look at the attributes, attitudes, and mental strategies of winning traders. Secrets of success. A comparison of the mental approach of a winning trader with that of a losing or mediocre trader.

Chapter Three
THE RELENTLESS POWER OF BELIEFS

Beliefs that winning traders hold. Three essential beliefs to effective trading. Ways to discover one's own beliefs. Steps for changing limiting beliefs and installing winning beliefs.

Chapter Four
EMOTIONS: THE WELLSPRING OF TRADING SUCCESS AND FAILURE

The vital importance of emotions. Emotions as valuable messengers. Ways to transform crippling emotions to empowering emotions. A new look at the fear and greed equation. A balancing act.

Chapter Five
CONFLICT RESOLUTION

How mixed messages mutilate profits. The importance of values. Getting things straight. Putting ideas into allignment. Discovering one's own core outcomes.

Chapter Six
CLARITY OF VISION AND
MARKET ASSESSMENT

Letting the market dictate the terms and turns. Becoming partners with the market. Wanting what the market wants. Releasing self-deception. The dangers of scenario trading. Gaining perspective.

Chapter Seven
IMAGINATION VERSUS WILL POWER

Why will power isn't enough. Learning to direct the imagination towards the probabilities. Imagining the success of a trade. Training the mind for optimism. Daydreams for the future. Building a vision.

Chapter Eight
UNCOUPLING YOUR EGO

Egoless trading. Building boundaries between oneself and ones trading. The difference between walls, no boundaries and healthy boundaries. Becoming more than the trading.

Chapter Nine
REPROGRAMING THE
SOFTWARE OF THE MIND

Directing attention and focus. Using power questions. A new approach to affirmations. Positive worry. Taking control of self-talk. Rewriting your script. Using the trading trance for success. Self-hypnosis.

Chapter Ten
THE PHYSIOLOGY OF EXCELLENCE

Physiology: the short cut to power trading. Posture. Breathing. Facial expression. Anchoring kinesthetically for calm and confidence. The quieting reflex. The relaxation response. The importance of exercise and nutrition.

Chapter Eleven
YOUR OFFICE

The importance of environment. Taking control. Power suggestions for floor traders. Cleaning out clutter. Setting up for success. Screen and phone placement. Electromagnetic considerations. Air cleansing. Lighting. Sounds. Feng Shui. Privacy.

Chapter Twelve
THE CONFIDENT TRADER

Trading in trust. Handling drawdowns. Turning failure into feedback. Using mistakes to grow. Developing consistency. Trading rules or guidelines. The evolution of better and better. Serenity Prayer

12 Habitudes of Highly Successful Traders

The mental aspect of trading contributes more to the success or failure of a trader than the system used, the rules employed, or any other factor. This important book discusses in detail twelve habitudes (habits and attitudes) that are vital to trading success and teaches you how to develop the mental and emotional skills essential to successful trading.

These habits and attitudes are:

- Preparedness
- Detachment
- Willingness to Accept Loss
- Taking Controlled Risk
- Thinking in Probabilities
- Being Comfortable with Uncertainty
- Consciousness of Abundance
- Optimism
- Open Mindedness and Clarity of Thought and Perception
- Courage
- Discipline

Author Ruth Barrons Roosevelt is, perhaps, better qualified to teach these essential traits to successful trading, since she herself has not only been an active trader for many years, but also has worked for many years with traders as a trading coach, helping them to overcome the psychological and emotional barriers to their trading success. She shows them, and she shows and teaches you through this excellent book how to develop the necessary attitudes to win consistently in the trading game. It outlines remarkable methods for developing internally the mental skills essential to winning in an arena where the majority of participants fail.

Order your copy today on our website, http://www.traderspress.com. The specific address where this book may be found is http://www.traderspress.org/detail.asp?product id=1840. You may also order by calling Traders Press, the publisher, at 800-927-8222.

VIEW OF TABLE OF CONTENTS FOR
12 HABITUDES OF HIGHLY SUCCESSFUL TRADERS

INTRODUCTION
THE HABITUDES

An overview of the habitudes. Self-test on the twelve habitudes.

CHAPTER ONE
THE HABITUDE OF PREPAREDNESS

Psychological preparation. Strategic preparation. Position sizing and money management. Data and information. Commitment to trading. Goal setting technique.

CHAPTER TWO
THE HABITUDE OF DETACHMENT

The issue of identity. Focus on the process. Creating Boundaries. Perceptual positions, a new perspective. Rebuilding the ego. An anxiety cure.

CHAPTER THREE
THE HABITUDE OF WILLINGNESS TO ACCEPT LOSS

Simple cost of doing business. What is and is not your job. Expecting to win. The Impasse. Growing losses. A story of terrible trading. The need to think differently. Resistance to loss can create loss. Overcoming resistance. Loss as feedback.

CHAPTER FOUR
THE HABITUDE OF TAKING CONTROLLED RISK

The risktakers. Playing the odds. A lifestyle tendency. Excitement or fear. Control. Flow. Individual differences.

CHAPTER FIVE
THE HABITUDE OF THINKING IN PROBABILITIES

The wildness lies in wait. All we really have are probabilities. Guide of life. Scientific enhancements. Probabilities overcome self-doubt and condemnation. Keep you in a balanced frame of mind. Probabilities remove the ego. Probabilities as power.

CHAPTER SIX
THE HABITUDE OF BEING COMFORTABLE WITH UNCERTAINTY
An essential for trading. Finding the rich opportunity in the unknowable. Benefits of uncertainty. The need to be right. A story. The open mind. Asking the right questions. The art and excitement of the unknowable.

CHAPTER SEVEN
THE HABITUDE OF TAKING THE LONG TERM VIEW
An adult perspective. Balance and equanimity. Don't sweat the small stuff. Stop doing what doesn't work. Viewing drawdowns as temporary. Gaining clarity. An elusive concept that serves you.

CHAPTER EIGHT
THE HABITUDE OF ABUNDANCE CONSCIOUSNESS
Scarcity at the root of trading problems. Limited pie or unlimited abundance. Abundance and power to overcome setbacks. How scarcity effects trading. Breaking the profit ceiling. Valuing wealth. Affirming and focusing on abundance.

CHAPTER NINE
THE HABITUDE OF OPTIMISM
Optimistic about the future. An explanatory style. Optimistic traders. Pessimistic traders. Realistic in the present. The importance of the meaning we give events. EEC test. The ability to change.

CHAPTER TEN
THE HABITUDE OF OPEN MINDEDNESS AND CLARITY
OF THOUGHT AND PERCEPTION
The problem of bias. A matter of identity. Dangers of bias in trading. Some words as clues. Indicators as lie detectors. Value of feedback. The truth shall make you free.

CHAPTER ELEVEN
THE HABITUDE OF COURAGE
Creating an increased capacity for courage. Asking courageous questions. Courage: not recklessness. The importance of respect for all aspects of trading. The Hero's Journey.

CHAPTER TWELVE
THE HABITUDE OF DISCIPLINE
Education and control of the self. Integrity of thought and action. Setting goals and acting in support of them. Doing, not trying. Specific trading guidelines. Trading as an art and adventure. A balanced approach.

7 Secrets Every Commodity Trader Needs to Know (Mound)
A Complete Guide to Trading Profits (Paris)
A Professional Look at S&P Day Trading (Trivette)
A Treasury of Wall Street Wisdom (Editors: Schultz & Coslow)
Ask Mr. EasyLanguage (Tennis)
Beginner's Guide to Computer Assisted Trading (Alexander)
Channels and Cycles: A Tribute to J.M. Hurst (Millard)
Chart Reading for Professional Traders (Jenkins)
Commodity Spreads: Analysis, Selection and Trading Techniques (Smith)
Comparison of Twelve Technical Trading Systems (Lukac, Brorsen, & Irwin)
Complete Stock Market Trading and Forecasting Course (Jenkins)
Cyclic Analysis (J.M. Hurst)
Dynamic Trading (Miner)
Exceptional Trading: The Mind Game (Roosevelt)
Fibonacci Ratios with Pattern Recognition (Pesavento)
Futures Spread Trading: The Complete Guide (Smith)
Geometry of Markets (Gilmore)
Geometry of Stock Market Profits (Jenkins)
Harmonic Vibrations (Pesavento)
How to Trade in Stocks (Livermore & Smitten)
Hurst Cycles Course (J.M. Hurst)
Investing by the Stars (Weingarten)
It's Your Option (Zelkin)
Magic of Moving Averages (Lowry)
Market Rap: The Odyssey of a Still-Struggling Commodity Trader (Collins)
Planetary Harmonics of Speculative Markets (Pesavento)
Point & Figure Charting (Aby)
Point & Figure Charting: Commodity and Stock Trading Techniques (Zieg)
Private Thoughts From a Trader's Diary (Pesavento & MacKay)
Profitable Patterns for Stock Trading (Pesavento)
RoadMap to the Markets (Busby)
Short-Term Trading with Price Patterns (Harris)
Single Stock Futures: The Complete Guide (Greenberg)
Stock Patterns for Day Trading (2 volumes) (Rudd)
Stock Trading Techniques Based on Price Patterns (Harris)
Technically Speaking (Wilkinson)
Technical Trading Systems for Commodities and Stocks (Patel)
The Amazing Life of Jesse Livermore: World's Greatest Stock Trader (Smitten)
The Handbook of Global Securities Operations (O'Connell & Steiniger)
The Opening Price Principle: The Best Kept Secret on Wall Street (Pesavento & MacKay)
The Professional Commodity Trader (Kroll)
The Taylor Trading Technique (Taylor)
The Trading Rule That Can Make You Rich* (Dobson)
Top Traders Under Fire (Collins)
Trading Secrets of the Inner Circle (Goodwin)
Trading S&P Futures and Options (Lloyd)
Twelve Habitudes of Highly Successful Traders (Roosevelt)
Understanding Bollinger Bands (Dobson)
Understanding Fibonacci Numbers (Dobson)
Viewpoints of a Commodity Trader (Longstreet)
Winning Edge 4 (Toghraie)
Winning Market Systems (Appel)

**Please contact Traders Press to receive our current catalog describing these and
many other books and gifts of interest to investors and traders.
800-927-8222 ~ 864-298-0222 ~ fax 864-298-0221
http://www.traderspress.com ~ e-mail ~ customerservice@traderspress.com**

Trader's Gift Shop

Market-related art available through

Traders Press, Inc.®

Varied selections of market-related
artwork and gifts are
available exclusively through
Traders Press, Inc.®
Currently available items are pictured on
our website at
http://www.traderspress.com and in our Traders Catalog,
which is available FREE upon request

You can contact us at:
800-927-8222 ~ 864-298-0222
Fax 864-298-0221

Traders Press, Inc.®
PO Box 6206
Greenville, SC 29606

Serving Traders Since 1975

Notes

Notes

Notes

Notes